brilliant colour at home

brilliant colour at

home

elizabeth hilliard

photography by ray main

kyle cathie limited

for William and Hugh

First published in Great Britain in 1999 by
Kyle Cathie Limited
20 Vauxhall Bridge Road
London SW1V 2SA

ISBN 1 85626 328 2

Text © 1999 Elizabeth Hilliard
Photography © 1999 Ray Main/Mainstream
Stylist: Karina Garrick
Design: Paul Welti
Editor: Kate Oldfield
Editorial assistant: Sheila Boniface
Copy editor: Catherine Ward

A CIP catalogue record for this title is available from the
British Library

Printed and bound in Singapore by Tien Wah Press

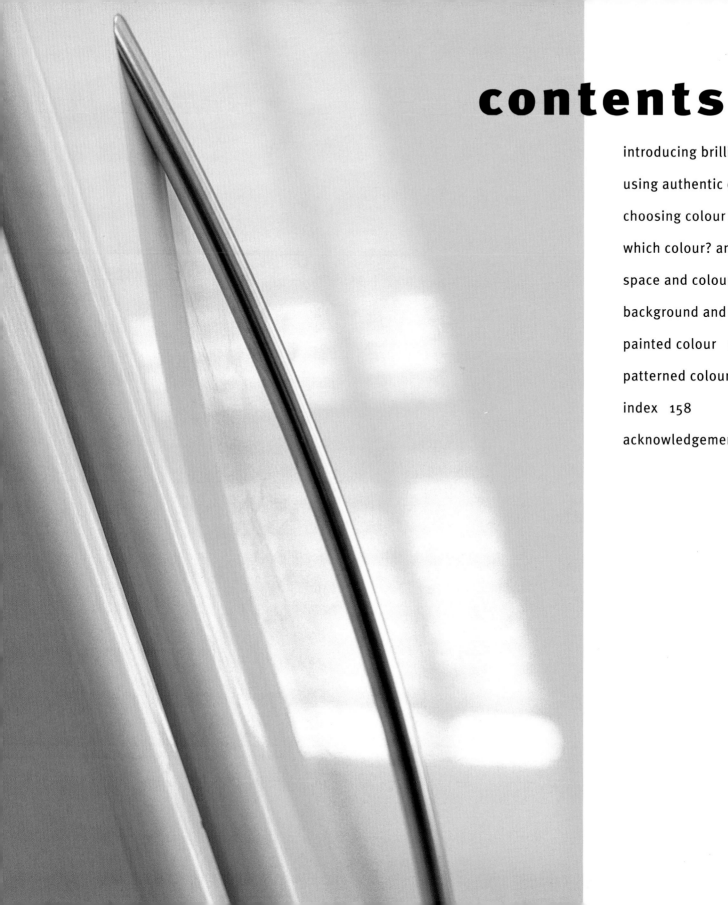

contents

don't be afraid ❏ what is bright colour? ❏ learning to love saturated colours

❏ compatible colours ❏ brilliant colour is memorable and fun

introducing brilliant colour

what colour can do for you ❏ colour and healing ❏

gem therapy ❏ india – queen of colour ❏ a world of colour ❏ colour and symbolism

If you are reading this book you are probably either already a convert to using bright colour to decorate your home, or you are open to conversion. One of the great decorating conundrums, if you know the joys of bright colour, is why so many people resist its allure or are afraid of using it. No-one, after all, would suggest that a garden is strange or unusual because it is full of brilliant clear blues, pinks, yellows and reds, all set against lush, verdant shades of bright green. On the contrary, it is exactly the freshness and vibrancy of these colours – combined, of course, as in decorating, with a degree of structure – that delight the eye and uplift the spirit. A garden is a visual feast, so why can't a home be?

nothing to be scared of

The reasons why bright colour can seem alarming are various. If you have grown up surrounded by muted tones within a narrow range, such as beige and sage green, bright colour can come as a visual shock. But what a shock! A shock that is invigorating, enlivening, both to the eye and to one's general feeling of well-being. If muted and pastel colours seem safe and brilliant colour risky – take a risk!

Jazzy cushions on a sofa (left).
Regal red and purple and fiery
orange glow against the
sapphire blue. These jewel-like
colours are given a lift by a
single citrus green cushion and
a couple of black-and-whites

The colours chosen for the
sofa cushions opposite are
drawn from this coffee
table (left) which has four
stained MDF lids, each with
storage beneath. Raffia
coasters continue the
theme. A traditional
squashy armchair (above)
is updated by being covered
in bright orange cotton.
The other colours complete
the look

Today, paint in particular of all decorating materials is relatively cheap, widely available and easy to change. If you make a mistake, so what – you can put it right. Do some looking and planning (described in **which colour? and why?**, pages 56–77) and you probably won't make the mistake in the first place. It's worth taking the risk to reap the benefits.

Then there is the fear that brilliant colour is somehow too much to live with, too overwhelming. The answer to this is that you don't have to decorate your entire home or even a whole room with bright colour, though once you have started you may find this is exactly what you want to do. If you are feeling tentative, start with a small room, freshen it up with a background of white or a pale shade of a clean colour and introduce touches of bright colour in cushions, pictures or posters, a vase, a tablecloth or a sofa throw. Or you can paint just part of a room– one wall, for example.

Another worry is that bright colour will be too dark. This usually arises from a misunderstanding about the difference between 'bright' and 'strong' colour, and confusion about the terminology in general. This book explains the jargon which is interesting but not actually necessary to the home decorator.

learning to love saturated hues

The main concept to grasp is that 'bright' colour means the pure pink or blue or whatever, with no black or white added. Bright colours can be strong, but they are fresh. They do not include shades like bottle green and burgundy red which are, indeed, dark – dark because they either have black mixed into the pure, bright colour, or they have been muddied by the mixture of pigments. Another point to remember is that the darkness or lightness of a room depends as much upon available natural light and how you use artificial lighting as on the brightness of the colour in which it is decorated.

Too much of a good thing? Some people might find this room overwhelming because it is so busy. A collection of elaborate objects can be pulled together with one dominant bright colour or a few related tones; while areas of white or a neutral help to relax a room

Suspicion of bright colour sometimes has its source in convention, an idea that it is somehow not socially acceptable, more than a little vulgar. This is another misunderstanding. It is, of course, possible to use bright orange, pink or green in a way that is kitsch or outrageous. But interiors that use brilliant colour can also be outstandingly elegant. Simplicity is the key. Vulgarity – which can in itself be fun and liberating – springs from the way the colour is used, not the colours themselves.

bright colour is not a fad

'Bright colour doesn't go with things' is something we often hear, and in a way this is a good point. It depends, though, on what colour the 'things' are. Any colour you use to decorate a room has to be compatible with the others, otherwise there will be a sense of unease, a visual jarring. Any colour has a group of other colours with which it looks good – place an earthy terracotta alongside a modern shocking pink and you could, indeed, be dissatisfied. As a general rule, bright colours go well with other bright colours, with white (which shows off their brilliance), with neutrals and grey (which subdue them somewhat), with some dark colours such as navy blue and deep scarlet (so long as the colour balance is right) and with pale shades produced by diluting the bright colours with white.

Brilliant colour is the most natural thing in the world, all over the world. Nature provides us with wonderful examples of bright colour; man adds the contrasts with his paintbrush

A popular misconception about bright colour is that it is a fad, a fashion that will pass and leave your home looking dated. Nothing could be further from the truth. Throughout history and across the world, bright colour has been sought and embraced as a powerful, life-enhancing medium, from primitive times onwards (see **using authentic colour**, pages 22–31). In the twentieth century, colour has simply become more colourfast, more available and brighter, as a result of technological advances. The new millennium will no doubt bring further colourful delights.

Bright colour is memorable in a way that drab colour is not. In the 1970s there was an experiment in which a group of people lived for a year in a village intended to replicate an iron age settlement. One of the things the inhabitants missed was colour and this is hardly surprising. Likewise, at least one of the men who was held hostage in the Middle East in the 1990s has recalled his yearning for colour during those terrible dark years.

colour and healing

Before the Enlightenment, the 'Age of Reason', in the eighteenth century, when logic and proof became the linchpins of philosophy and scientific thinking, colour had a part to play both in healing and, in some parts of the world, the worship of deities. Even after the Enlightenment, ideas about the healing powers of colour persisted. Edwin Babbitt was an interesting proponent of these theories, which he published in his book, *The Principles of Light and Colour*, in 1878. Babbitt said that different colours affect different parts of the human body. Yellow, he believed, stimulated the nervous system and helped to relieve constipation and bronchial congestion, while blue was calming and anti-inflammatory, useful in treating migraines, sunstroke and sciatica. Red was a stimulant for the blood and could be used to help those suffering from paralysis, exhaustion and stiff joints.

Ideas like these that link healing with colour persist into the present age, to some extent because a number of people have found relief through colour therapy. Though conventional clinical medicine does not generally recognise colour healing as valid, some forms of it are nonetheless used routinely. Neonatal jaundice in babies, which as recently as the 1960s was treated with blood transfusions, is now treated by placing the baby (with eyes shielded) under bright blue light. Claims are also made that the same blue light helps sufferers of rheumatoid arthritis.

A simple blue staircase (left) climbs a wall that has been roughly rendered then painted green in the cottage home of designer Mary Rose Young.

Rich and fiery colours are energising. As a background, they bring warmth to the objects they display – useful if the objects are themselves monochrome or neutral. Red seems an appropriate backdrop to the mischief expressed in this South American mask

india – queen of colour

One particular type of colour healing is practised in India and known as gem therapy. This discipline is based on the belief that gemstones store cosmic energies which relate to the individual energies in everyone. Gem Therapists believe that different coloured gems can be used to cure and prevent illness. Coloured gems are burnt and the ash is taken by the patient, or the stones are steeped in alcohol to absorb the energy and then administered in small quantities.

India is, of course, a country of brilliant colour. Red, blue, green, yellow, purple... brilliance of every hue can be seen in the jewel-like colours of the saris worn by women in the south to the hibiscus garlands sold near the Kali Temple in Calcutta in the east, to the multicoloured stained glass in the grand buildings of Jodhpur in the west, to the rainbow colours of bunting and tents at a Ladakh festival in the north.

As a source of inspiration for using bright colour, India is queen, although almost every hot country in the world seems to use intense colours quite naturally – something to do with the light, perhaps, and the fact that such colours themselves have a 'hot' quality.

the indian festival of holi

Perhaps the most thrilling, to an outsider, of all aspects of India's dazzling use of colour is the once-yearly rainbow anarchy that is the Hindu festival of Holi. On every street corner a makeshift stall sells powder of every colour. Though the traditional colour is red, called 'gulal', today the powder is as likely to be pink, green purple, yellow... the more vibrant and shocking, the better. People of all ages, but especially the young, roam the streets or ambush friends and throw over them their

supplies of coloured powder, making brothers and sisters almost unrecognisable, their faces and clothes caked in brilliant colour. Holi heralds the spring, its lack of inhibition and its celebration of brilliant colour reflecting the imminent explosion of leaves and flowers across the landscape and in gardens everywhere. The story in which the festival has its origin is one of good triumphing over evil – naturally, good is represented by the life-enhancing colours with which Holi is celebrated.

the colours of the world

Part of the pleasure of travelling is having the opportunity to observe and absorb the colours of countries other than our own. Another country which seems always to be bathed in colour is Greece. Brilliant blue

Colour enlivens the outside of buildings too, and not only traditional or ethnic structures. These contemporary urban houses in Australia use blocks of scarlet for visual impact

is the colour most often associated with Greece – the blue of Mediterranean sea and sky in summer, which evokes oregano-scented hillsides, the gentle tonk-tonk of roaming sheep's bells and the sound of waves lapping the shore. Setting off this blue's intensity is the chalky dazzle of lime-washed buildings in village streets.

Of course, Greece is a country of many colours, not just blue. Kalymnos, one of the islands of the Dodecanes, off Turkey, is famous for the rainbow colours in which the outsides of the houses are painted, neighbours choosing different shades to contrast with each other. The effect is delightful.

Many other places besides the Greek Islands have a tradition of painting their house-fronts varying colours – Bermuda, Mexico and Haiti, for example. Murano, the island in the Venetian lagoon famous for producing the finest hand-blown glass and hand-made lace, is a riot of colour. The effect is enhanced by the inhabitants' choice of vibrant striped curtains and the occasional red or blue chair left outside the front of the house, where the occupant had been sitting enjoying the sunshine only a minute before.

The villages of West Cork in Ireland have a similar tradition, which shows that the drive for colour is not entirely confined to hot climates. Here, each shop is painted a different shade, with the board on which the proprietor's name is displayed often painted in matching brilliant yellow or blue, for example. Some of the buildings are more pastel than brilliant – a concession perhaps to the climate.

the importance of context

Of course, not all brilliant colours are attractive in all situations. There are particularly intense, harsh shades of blue and green, for example, that look stunning in the hot sun of the Mediterranean or the Indian subcontinent but which, if you transport them home to less sunny climes, suddenly look cold and sad. Brilliant does not necessarily mean beautiful. This is why learning to look at colours in your own home and in your local environment, taking into account the quality of the natural light, is important as well as enjoyable (see **which colour? and why?**, pages 56–77 for more about this).

Fabric samples and paint sample pots are immensely helpful in the quest for the *right* bright colour. The editor of a decorating magazine recently said that she thought sample pots were the single most important invention in home decorating in recent decades and she may be right – they are undoubtedly liberating, as is the huge and expanding range of paint colours and types available today.

colour through the ages

Throughout history, bright colour has been a powerful way of communicating ideas. This is especially true in areas where the population is largely illiterate, so that visual messages have added significance. If you were a peasant living in the countryside around a cathedral city in medieval England, for example, your daily existence, surroundings and expectations of life could be routinely grim and grey. Go into the cathedral, however, and you would see the glory of God and His angels – as well as the Judgement and the fate of the damned – described in the stained glass. You would receive the message loud and clear, especially when the colours were fired up by rays of sunshine. Salvation and heaven would definitely be worth striving for in this context, a message perhaps lost, or mislaid, in today's colourful and relatively luxurious homes.

colour and symbolism

Colour has always held symbolic meaning. Take red, for example, a visually powerful colour frequently connected with the emotions and passions. Other associations for red are danger, courage and virility. Priapus, the Phrygian god of fertility, was portrayed as an ugly man with disproportionately large genitals. Known as the 'red god', he was also the deity of gardens, bees, sheep and goats. Red can also refer to illicit sex, as in the 'red light district' and the 'scarlet woman'.

In parts of China and India, red is associated with the marriage ceremony, an indicator that the woman is embarking upon what she (and the two families) hope will be a fruitful period of her life. Red symbolises martyrdom for faith, or defiance of existing powers, both in history and in more recent centuries. The Red Army was the Bolshevik force which overthrew the power of the Tsars and the 'white' Russians in the early decades of the twentieth century. Red was the colour linked to Mars, the god of war. In Ghana in western Africa, meanwhile, the 'kobene' is a special cloth that mourners closely related to a dead person wrap around themselves. The brilliance of the kobene's red is dazzling, but in this country and context it is the colour of sorrow.

Blue and green are cool, calm colours, suggesting serenity and spirituality. In Christianity, the Virgin Mary is usually shown dressed in blue, and blue is the colour frequently associated with the mother figure or queen of heaven in other religions. Blue is, of course, the colour of the sky and thus suggestive of remoteness, expansive space and boundlessness. If red shouts out blood and warfare, blue and green whisper peace.

Green is, of course, the colour of life. In various religions it is associated with faith, immortality and the resurrection, or life after death. In the Christian faith, green is the colour linked with Easter, new growth and the season of spring. Green is half way through the colour spectrum and is therefore considered the colour of harmony or balance. In the home, it is supposed to have antiseptic qualities – country kitchens were often painted green because the colour was believed to repel flies.

Across countries and cultures, purple has for centuries been the symbol of authority. It is a serious colour, suggesting solemnity and stateliness. Purple is the colour of bishops in the Christian church. To purple, a fusion of red and blue, can be ascribed the qualities of both those other colours – physical prowess with nobility and spirituality – an impressive combination. The reason why purple has this reputation may be attributable to a purely practical source – the rarity of the dye until the nineteenth century. Derived from a Mediterranean sea snail, the dye was not only expensive beyond reason but difficult to handle – two soakings in different types of solution were required to achieve true 'Tyrian' purple, the colour of the Roman emperors' robes. The recipe for this dye has been lost.

In the spectrum of colour healing, there is no purple. Instead, it is replaced with violet and magenta, the former corresponding to spiritual awareness and insight, the latter to release ideas and events in our past that are holding us back from growth and development.

Yellows and oranges are powerful too. The most obvious association for yellow is with the sun, bringing life and colour and lifting our spirits.

bold vivid colour

These colours that evoke such strong ideas and associations, are not wishy-washy shades but intense, bold colours. Bright red and blue, green and purple are not new but they are sometimes overlooked. The advent of the new millennium is a good time to rediscover them, use them to bring their life and joy into our homes and lives. Bright colour without fuss or frills is today's and tomorrow's decorating language.

**Luxurious ferny greens
induce a lush, cool mood**

say it with flowers

We need look no further than a flower
bed (or shop) for drop-dead beautiful
colours. From far right: the brilliance
of ranunculus, tulips, anemones and
more tulips with chrysanthemums

There is a growing interest in authentic colour. The word 'authentic' has been in danger of being overused, but it has not quite yet lost its impact. Its literal meaning is 'genuine' or 'the real thing'. In the context of interior decoration, it suggests that the colour is honest, in keeping with its origins and use.

what is authentic colour?

Historic colours are 'authentic' in this sense, because they contain earth and other natural pigments and materials to produce paint in colours and with finishes that are as near as possible to those which would have been originally applied. But authentic colour is not only historical. It applies equally to national and ethnic styles and to the many exciting developments in colour technology in the past fifty years or so.

There is a danger in thinking that all historic colours are drab, but this is far from being the case. Brilliant colour has been used throughout history, in many countries and societies, always depending upon the ability to make pigments. People of fashion decorated their homes with bright colours whenever they could afford to, because the expense of the pigments demonstrated their status – quite apart from the sheer pleasure of living with them. In some cases the original colours changed, because the pigments used were volatile or fugitive. As a result, mistakes have been made in researching the layers of paint on walls and furniture – it is possible, for example, that the 'Gustavian' grey, much used today to reproduce the Scandinavian style of painted furniture, was actually the undercoat to other, more distinctive, colours.

This beautiful blue, reminiscent of sunny skies and sea, is actually to be found in one of the servants' departments, the bakehouse, at the English stately home of Lanhydrock in Cornwall. It was cheap and easy to make with the same pigment (sometimes known as 'dolly blue') used for whitening laundry

Glorious golden yellow at Claydon House, Buckinghamshire, England.
In the middle of the eighteenth century Claydon was redecorated by the
Verney family in the fashionable chinoiserie style – hence the carved
and painted wooden birds and flowers romping across this chimney
breast in the North hall

Yellow ochre was a wonderful rich yellow and possibly the most widely available of the natural earth pigments, but king's or chrome yellow, when you could obtain and afford them, were much brighter and more prominent, both visually and socially. Never mind that king's yellow was highly poisonous, consisting of arsenic trisulphide – in those days it was not the owners who applied the paint (and in any case, since its toxicity was well known, it would no doubt have been handled with care).

Claydon House, a stately home in Buckinghamshire in England, dating back in parts to the forteenth-century, owned for 350 years by the Verney family and now in the possession of the National Trust, was completely overhauled and redecorated during the 1750s. This included much ornate chinoiserie and many brilliant colours, including king's yellow and blue verditer, the latter derived from copper carbonate as a bright by-product of silver production. The drawing room of Sir John Soane's house at Lincoln's Inn Fields in London was also famously decorated in bright yellow in 1813 – not only were the walls yellow, but so were the upholstery and curtains, both edged in red.

The eighteenth and early nineteenth century enthusiasm for bright colour stemmed from an interest in the arts, architecture and interior decoration of ancient Greece and Rome. Wealthy young men travelled across Europe and brought home paintings and artefacts. If they could afford him, they would then employ Robert Adam to remodel and redecorate their family homes. These ideas crossed the Atlantic to the eastern seaboard of North America. Homewood House in Baltimore, with its bright pea-green hallway and blue drawing room, illustrates this communication of ideas.

Brass bed and lamps contribute to the glow of this contemporary Indian interior decorated in brilliant marigold yellow. Touches of red on the bed and curtains add spice

Bright yellow used in quantity is always dramatic. Claude Monet's dining room in his house at Giverny outside Paris in France, now open to the public, is a memorable example of this. In the twentieth century, a yellow room which caused a sensation was Nancy Lancaster's drawing room in London. Owner of the interior decoration firm Colefax and Fowler, she chose the colour in the 1950s when England was still recovering from war-time rationing and dreariness. Walls, curtains, furnishings, even the Ukrainian rug on the floor, were all yellow. There was also a fair quantity of white and areas of reddish pink – on the spines of books, vases and other accessories, as well as the covering of some of the chairs.

The vast quantity of historical colours, however, and certainly those used by less wealthy members of the population, were more earthy in tone, consisting of yellows, reds, browns and brownish-greens. Many of the historic paint colours marketed today have a similarly wonderful, earthy depth to them which is part of the reason they live happily in old houses. This quality gives them a certain subtlety that does not lend them to co-existence with brilliant colours. Of course, this is not true of all colours in the manufacturers' historic or 'heritage' ranges. You will find that some of these colours, especially the yellows, are bright enough in themselves to be used alongside contemporary brilliant colour. Others, such as the chalky whites and greys, can provide useful background colour.

Fashions in colour come and go, and often they come around again and again, decades or even centuries later. An obscure but delightful volume called *The Laws of Harmonious Colouring* was written by the little known David Ramsay Hay and published in several editions in the early nineteenth century. His words are music to today's lover of bright colour.

colour theories

Hay was English, and everyone knows that it rarely stops raining in England. He was all for counteracting dreariness with bright colour in decorating. 'Until very lately,' he writes, 'white, neutral hues, and pale tints of colour only were used... a practice that it is difficult at first view to account for in a country like this, where we are, by a variable climate, denied the study and enjoyment of nature's colouring for many days in every season of the year; and must, consequently, content ourselves with what the interior decorations of our dwellings afford.'

Then he launches the attack. 'This vapid tameness in the colouring of our dwellings' he declares, 'is... inexcusable.' He deplores the fashion for one insipid colour one season, another the next, such as salmon, sage, drab and slate. Hay holds particular scorn for people who are too timid or polite to dare to

A sensuous east-meets-west bedroom, a crimson cave lit with oriental paper lanterns

use colour creatively. 'People of refinement' he says, 'have a disinclination to colours. This may be owing partly to weakness of sight, partly to the uncertainty of taste, which readily takes refuge in absolute negation.' His words may seem comic today, especially with reference to the need for spectacles, but there may be more than a grain of truth in the idea that there are 'polite' colours.

bold ethnic usage

Ethnic colour, as used by people in the tropics and Africa, is very far from polite. It is bright, it seems to vibrate from friction with the bright colours next to it, whether painted onto the exterior of a building or embroidered and appliquéd onto textiles and costumes. In Mexico or Morocco, in the scarlet robes of an Indian monk, the colourful shelving on the wall of a South African home or on the brilliantly contrasting Haitian window shutters, ethnic colour has a rawness that is thrilling to the jaded northern eye, depressed (as Hay pointed out) by too many grey winter days. It is enough to make one want to jump on the next plane out.

Ethnic colour is often historic, in the sense that it has been used for hundreds of years to decorate the natural materials from which homes, possessions, carts and boats are constructed, and to protect them from the elements – in particular the searing heat of the sun.

In stark contrast to the warmth and vibrancy of the tropics, Europe was launched into a wave of drabness with the onset of the Second World War (1939–45). The energies of industry and

Areas of flat bright primaries look stunning in a predominantly white setting. This page has been designed to echo paintings by Piet Mondrian (1872-1944) whose severe geometric style and use of colour was once revolutionary and has since influenced everything from interiors to advertising

design was limited by and channelled into the requirements of war. A generation of young people grew up with 'make do and mend', the availability of just about everything being subject to rationing.

It was not until the 1950s that European designers and industry were able to use colour again. Some of the ideas of using flat, bright colour originated from art movements of earlier decades (the Bauhaus and De Stijl, for example), but the war interrupted these possibilities, at the same time allowing a hiatus during which ideas could mature.

design movements

The Bauhaus is credited with introducing flat, bright colour to the modern home. An art school in Weimar in Germany established in 1919 and later moved to Dessau, the Bauhaus practised the concept of the unity of design, inspired by William Morris of the English Arts and Crafts movement of the later nineteenth-century. Artists, craftsmen, designers and architects worked together towards a style that was modern, of its age, using modern ideas and materials. The discovery, at about this time, that titanium dioxide could provide a widely available, good-quality white paint contributed both to the all-white look adopted by the modernists, and to the use of bright colour, since the white gave it a clean foundation and dazzling contrast. In 1933, however, the Nazis closed the school.

It's not only in smart urban houses that blocks of bright colour are at home. This is architect John Pardey's striking family home in the English countryside

De Stijl was the stylistic umbrella for many forward-looking artists and designers, including Piet Mondrian. Mondrian is famous for his paintings such as *Broadway Boogie-Woogie* (1942–3), which uses a grid of black lines on a white background with spaces filled with blocks of bright primary colours.

influence of fifties' design

1950s designers of Scandinavian glass and American textiles were among the leaders in using brilliant colour in a way that startled the post-war public. The 'Ravenna' bowls, which Sven Palmqvist had been developing since 1948, were inspired by the Byzantine mosaics at Ravenna in Italy and encased pieces of coloured glass in the walls of glass bowls where they glowed with the brilliance of stained glass.

The American furniture manufacturer Knoll caused a sensation in the later 1950s by using fabric which shockingly juxtaposed orange and pink. Furniture designers like Charles Eames and George Nelson (designer of the famous Marshmallow sofa of 1956) also favoured bright clashing colours for their textile cushions and upholstery.

Moulded plastic chairs (and other plastic items) were made in a collection of different bright colours. Some of these designs, in particular those by Robin Day for Hille, are still in production today. If you are lucky enough to own or find original 1950s plastic furniture or objects (or 'plastics', as the experts call them), treat them with as much care as you would any other antique, rather than as you would a modern plastic item.

The idea of mix-and-match was widely developed in the 1950s. This was another 'modern' concept that freed you from having to buy an inflexible 'set' of matching chairs, or a complete china dinner or tea service, as your parents and grandparents had done. Instead, you could make your own collection from a choice of identical forms which the manufacturers offered in different colourse.

A scheme to surprise traditionalists. Using what might be considered 'clashing' colours in a carefully checked balance with white as a binding agent, this apartment has been decorated to stunning effect

colour defines the decades

Each decade since the 1950s has used colour to define the look of the age, in all aspects of design including interior decoration. The typical 1960s interior used psychedelic combinations like yellow and orange or pink and purple, which signified the advent of the teenage revolution, the throwing off of conventional values, the arrival of the contraceptive pill. Another 1960s signature was black and white used together in a look that was inspired by Mary Quant, the queen of London's King's Road, credited with inventing the mini skirt.

In the 1970s, bright colour took a back seat to sludgy browns, greens and creams, and the 1980s were characterised by chintz and florals, alongside a preoccupation with pastels and clever paint finishes like rag-rolling and faux marble.

The 1990s was the age of choice. Texture was rediscovered, and so was minimalism, its ideological edges softened by sensual luxuries like fleece throws (polyester 'polar' fleece, that is, though sheepskins were OK too), cashmere-covered cushions, wall-to-wall sound and non-stop affordable high-tech central heating to take the chill off the bare floor. You could go 'simple' (paint everything white, unless it was dark brown), 'makeover' (a wonderful jumble of colours and shapes), or 'historic' (rich colours, distemper and lime-wash and Persian rugs). What was important was that you were true to yourself and your taste. The catchphrase of the 1990s was: 'The choice is yours!'

busting through the jargon ❑ theories ❑ the colour wheel ❑ primaries, secondaries
and tertiaries ❑ complementaries ❑ how to use the colour wheel at home

choosing colour schemes

where in the home? ❑ colour combinations ❑

clashing colours ❑ mixing new and old ❑ children's rooms ❑ colourful inspiration

This is the moment of truth. You like the idea of using bright colour and you are looking forward to living

with it. The problem is, where do you start? Where and how do you begin to turn your aspirations into

practical reality? Most people need time to look and plan before they pick up a paintbrush or call in the

decorator. This is time well spent. Indeed, there is no point rushing into things if you are not ready. The

weeks or months in which you build up a vision of your home can be a revelation, a time of pure pleasure

when you have the opportunity to wallow in bright colour and discover the colour schemes you really

want in your home.

busting through the jargon

There are many words that are used to describe colour in the home – from general words like comple-

mentary, toning and clashing to the more technical ones that enable professionals to talk to each other

about the minutiae of their subject. As always, jargon holds a certain fascination for the lay person.

Understanding it also means that you can't be baffled by it.

The nature of colour is a slippery idea and extremely difficult to describe. Paint manufacturers

struggle to give evocative names to their colours, sometimes to delightful or comic effect. Colour is

such a powerful and fascinating force, however, that scientists and observers have strived to pin down

its nature and effects from time immemorial.

Most colour jargon derives from colour science, the father of which Is the great Sir Isaac Newton,

the seventeenth-century physicist. In 1666 he made the astounding discovery that white light directed through the triangular form of a prism splits into an array of different colours. This is known as the spectrum. As defined by Newton, the colours that make up the spectrum are red, orange, yellow, green, blue, indigo and violet.

a short run through the science

Today, we take the spectrum for granted. The prism effect is demonstrated in every primary school and the light spectrum is a source of visual delight to adults and children alike when seen in nature (the rainbow) or in the home (when a ray of sunlight catches the edge of a bevelled mirror, for example).

Newton began a process of scientific colour analysis that continues today, but he was not the first to debate its qualities. Ancient thinkers, like Pythagoras, Plato and Aristotle, discussed it and Leonardo da Vinci considered its qualities in his *Treatise on Painting* (1651).

Michel-Eugène Chevreul, writing about colour in the mid-nineteenth century, was a hugely influential and remarkable man. His famous book *The Principles of Harmony and Contrast of Colours* was published in 1839. In it he examined various optical illusions based on the effects colours have on one another, especially when they are placed next to each other with no space in between. Through his book, Chevreul's ideas have had an enormous impact on modern art. The Impressionist artists were inspired to use colour more freely and positively than had ever been dared before. The shadows of objects painted out of doors came to life when enriched by the complementary of the colour of the object. Instead of trying to reproduce the exact appearance of a scene before them, artists aimed to paint the impression it gave, the way light and colour danced on a surface (especially water) when seen in full sunlight. The critics poured scorn on the results, but modern art was born.

The three most famous colour experts of the twentieth century were probably Wilhelm Ostwald, Albert Munsell and Faber Birren. More recently, the Danish designer Verner Panton championed bright colour through his lectures, books and futuristic designs until his death in 1998. 'Colours' he declared, 'can generate an echo in the soul and influence the entire body.'

The attempt to establish guidelines and a language for colour still continues today. Technically speaking, a 'tint' is a colour with white added while black added to a colour makes it a 'shade'. This can be confusing to the lay person, who generally uses the word 'shade' to help describe all the variations of a colour (as does this book) rather than colours which have been darkened by having black added. Thus (to you and me) lime and emerald are shades of green.

Likewise 'bright' is an ambiguous term, technically referring to the saturation or lightness of a tone, whereas in general usage it means a pure, strong colour as opposed to a pastel or dark colour. 'Tone', meanwhile, is understood by both technicians and by the lay person to mean the lightness or darkness of a single colour (pink being a pale tone of red).

'Metamerism' is an interesting word in the colour vocabulary. It refers to how surfaces that appear the same in natural light can be quite different when seen in artificial light. This is a significant consideration, and wherever possible is worth researching before finally deciding on materials for decorating.

the colour wheel

The 'colour wheel' is often referred to. Put simply, it provides a way of organising the colours of the spectrum so that they are visually accessible, by arranging them in a circle – the first (the reds) next to the last (the violets and purples). The three colours that are the basis of all pigments – red, yellow and blue – are placed at one-third intervals around this ring and are known as the 'primary' colours. At equal distances between these are the so-called 'secondaries', each composed of a mixture of the nearest two primaries. The 'tertiaries' are the colours between each of these first six. Thus the tertiary between red (primary) and orange (secondary, between red and yellow) is a reddish-orange.

The colour directly opposite any colour on the wheel is its 'complementary', the complementary of red being green and so on. A 'split complementary' is, technically speaking, an interesting three-way colour scheme which groups a colour on the wheel with the two tertiaries that neighbour its complementary. Orange would thus be used with two shades of blue, one greenish and one purplish. 'Triadic' is the term used for a colour scheme that uses three colours, all equidistant on the colour wheel.

There are, of course, too many tiny variations in colour to allow them all to appear on one wheel –

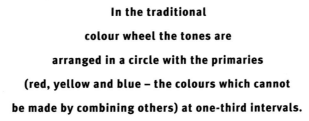

In the traditional
colour wheel the tones are
arranged in a circle with the primaries
(red, yellow and blue – the colours which cannot
be made by combining others) at one-third intervals.

the colour wheel

You can make your own colour 'wheel' using
bright shades you like cut from
paint manufacturers sample
cards, for example.

Contemporary interior
decoration sets us free to use
colour schemes traditionalists
might consider discordant or
clashing – reds and purples
together, for example, or
citrus yellows and greens

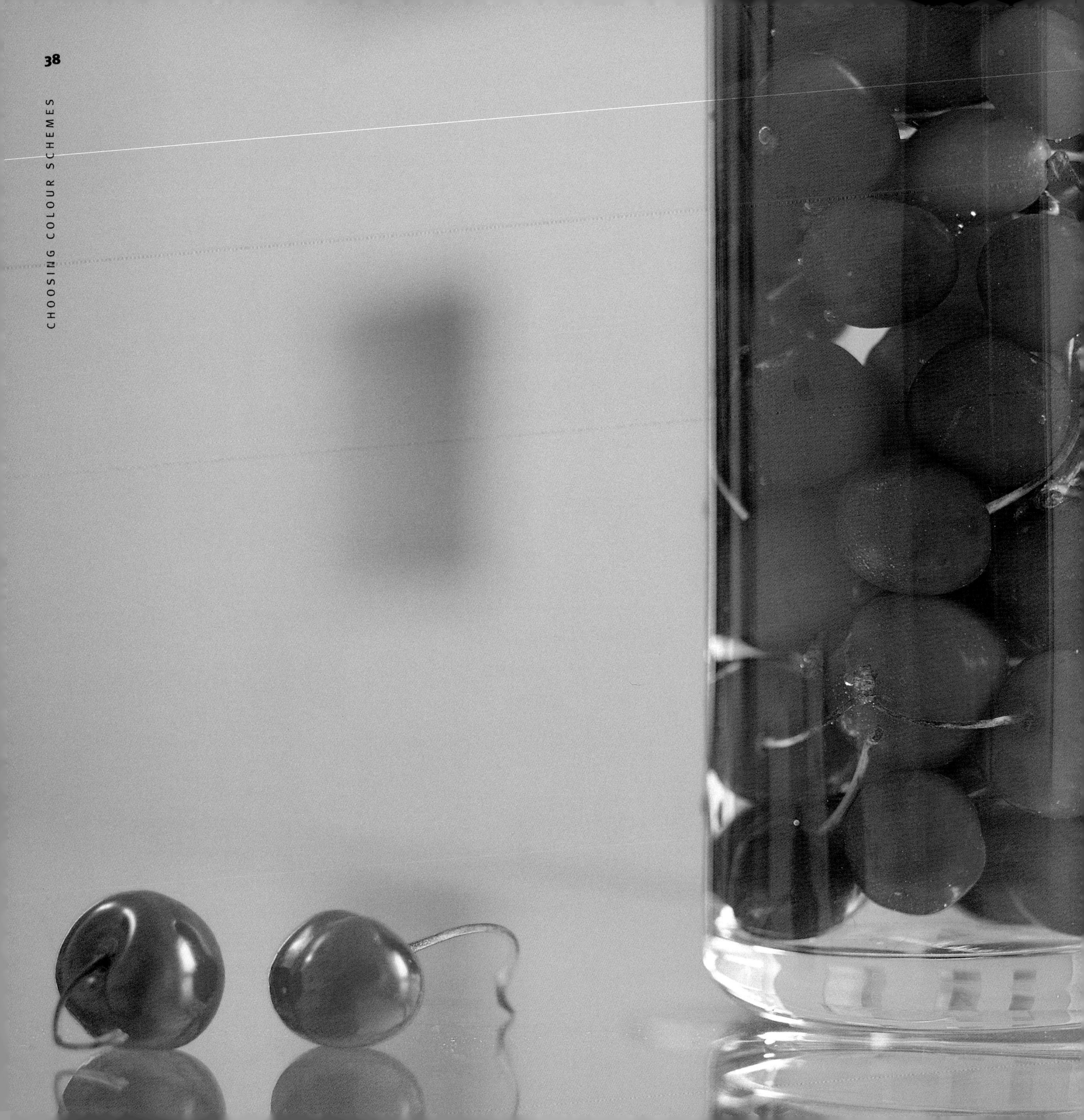

Red and green are complementaries, opposite each other on the colour wheel. Together they are strong, vibrant, creating a buzz that is thrilling to the eye. They can be used to balance each other, or accents of one can give the other an edge

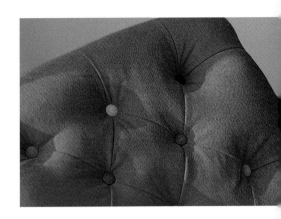

just look at the display of colour cards in a DIY store to get an idea of how subtle some variations are. The study of colour continues, although the technical accuracy of today's mass spectrometers, polarising microscopes and 'Standard Colours' have made much theorising redundant. The colour wheel is a useful device and no amount of science will deprive it of that status.

Traditional colour theory maintained that there were two types of colour scheme – those that were harmonised and those that were discordant. Harmonious schemes came in four types: monochromatic, achromatic, analogous and complementary. A 'monochromatic' scheme was one drawn from various shades of the same colour. The 'achromatic' colours were black, white, grey and silver – colours without colour, as it were. An 'analogous' scheme used colours near each other on the colour wheel, such as yellow and orange, and a 'complementary' scheme used colours opposite each other on the colour wheel.

colour schemes

All these schemes can be used today, but contemporary interior decoration also sets us free to use schemes that the traditionalists would have considered discordant or clashing, as well as neutrals in shades of cream and chocolate, the warm and sensual cousins of the rather chilly 'achromatic' scheme.

There are various ways you can use a colour wheel to help create a colour scheme for your home. Make your own selection of colours from around the spectrum, using only fresh, bright tones, and

A colour scheme to surprise traditionalists. Using what might be considered 'clashing' colours in a carefully checked balance with white as a binding agent, this apartment has been decorated to stunning effect

arrange them in a circle similar to the traditional colour wheel. If you take two of each colour card from the manufacturer's selection, you can paste one to your 'wheel', keeping the other on hand to try separately with other colours, rather than seeing them all together on the wheel.

dynamic combinations

Another approach is to choose two colours that are either at one-third intervals around the traditional wheel, such as red and blue, or are opposite each other (in which case they are complementaries such as purple and yellow). The result will be a bold, aggressive combination that has a primitive energy but is also potentially exhausting to live with. Such a combination could be dynamic in a kitchen or a children's playroom, but would not be ideal in a bedroom, unless it is used with subtlety and restraint.

Peppery reds and pinks are used in the interiors on these pages with splashes and touches of white and gold to highlight their brilliance. The result is electrifying rather than restful, so be careful which rooms you decorate with this hot, exotic colour combination

Purple and green – another pair of complementaries. Here the blue tones dominate, refreshed with touches of green in the fruit, vase and foliage

complimentaries

This use of complementary colours has not been particularly fashionable in the past decade, which has favoured instead a segmented approach to the colour wheel. Take a segment which covers any third of the wheel, like a large slice of cake. The range of colours in this tranche will be closely related (in other words 'clashing'). The result can be exciting, if the segment ranges from orange to pink, or soothing, if

Here the green is dominant, a touch of blue providing a focus and, by acting as a contrast, emphasising the luscious greenness of the green

it includes shades of blue moving towards green. This approach is also uniquely practical, because when you choose fabrics and accessories you are not under pressure to match exact tones.

An important fact to remember about the colour wheel is that it is only a device. It is merely a tool (albeit a useful one) to help you develop your own sense of colour relationships. Of course, you do not have to refer to it at all if you know what you want. If you have confidence in your judgement when seeking

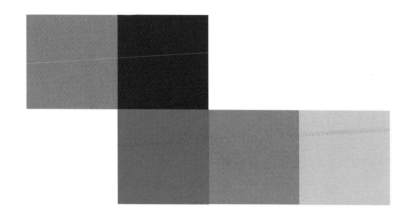

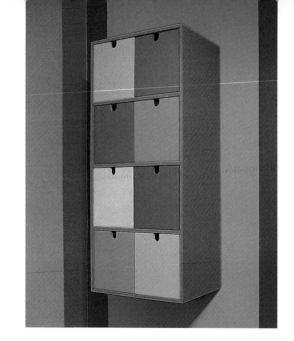

These colours (above and above right) are all drawn from one half of the colour wheel, from blue round to orange through purple. In the interior opposite, the pink of the room beyond designates a different living area, linked to the kitchen by the use of another shade of blue

solutions in interiors shops, don't feel tied to the colour wheel. Don't, in fact, feel tied to any particular theories. Feel free to use clashing colours like brilliant yellow, orange and pink together. Don't believe anyone who tells you that this combination is 'tasteless'. The result could be stunning if used on whole walls, for example, or piquant if used sparingly, perhaps in cushions on a white sofa.

Clashing colours create a frisson all their own. For this reason, think carefully about where to use them and how many to use together. Like complementary colours, they are dynamic and thrilling to the eye, but they can also be exhausting. Limit yourself to two or three initially.

The colours on these pages are again chosen from one half of the colour wheel, this time from purple to yellow, encompassing shades of orange and gold. The dominant purple creates a serious, magnificent mood and looks especially regal combined with gold and cheetah animal print fabric

An area of the house like a hallway, where you do not sit and look at the colours, could be a candidate for an all-over treatment in a startling palette. A large living room could also carry the impact of a clashing combination. If it is a rather dull, box-like room in a new house it might positively benefit from being transformed by this treatment. For best results, keep the colour in simple blocks unless you are purposely striving for an Op-art, psychedelic effect. For example, you could paint the end walls a different colour from the side walls (have these white or a fresh, pale colour), and have a third colour on the floor (lino, carpet, painted boards or concrete). Or you could dye your sofa and armchair covers in different, plain, clashing colours, such as purple, red and orange. So long as the walls are white, or possibly a clean, pale colour (white mixed with a little of one of your choice of colours), the effect will be brilliant rather than overwhelming.

using bold colour with paler shades

This brings us to a frequent question in connection with bright colour. Will other, less brilliant colours 'go' with it, or does white always have to be the accompanying colour? Background colour is discussed in greater detail on pages 100–119, but for now, it is possible to say that, yes, some other colours can live happily

Warm tones like these reds and burnt oranges bring a neutral interior to life. Many 'historic' tones go well with brilliant colour – such as the huge choice of whites and soft neutrals. The paint used on these walls is actually from a range of 'historic' paints, the National Trust colours, available from Farrow and Ball

alongside bright colours. Pale shades of bright colours work perfectly well and provide a comfortable background for bright colours. If you want a pale shade of green for the walls of your kitchen, to co-ordinate with a set of chairs that you have painted bright leafy green, for example, simply mix your own paint by adding a blob of your green to some white paint. If you are using a water-based emulsion for walls, find a water-based paint that matches your chairs and add a sample pot of this to the white.

When mixing your own paint in this way, be very careful to add colour only a little at a time – once in, you can't take it out. Make plenty of the mixture so that you will not have to make another batch, which probably won't be identical because the quantities may be minutely different. And remember to keep a note of what quantities you have used, just in case you do run out or want to try to reproduce the colour in years to come. Even if it is not an exact match, it will be approximately the same.

Colours that do not generally co-operate with bright colour are certain dark shades, pastels, some neutrals and most historic colours made from traditional materials. Dark colours like maroon and bottle or dark mossy green are likely to kill bright colour unless they are used in small areas. Sickly pastels like candy pink or peppermint green will introduce a note of discord if used in conjunction with bright colours. Drabs like mushroom brown or soft, sage green will simply look grubby, while the bright colours next to them will look like they have appeared from another planet. Historic colours made from traditional materials, as well as having an earthy quality, have a completely different surface appearance to modern paints (see **painted colour**, pages 120-137 for more about this) and so may not work well with them.

A popular concern about using bright colour is the question of deciding which colour to use in which room. There are various opinions on this, based on the psychology of colour. You do not, of course, have to follow these, though many of them are common sense.

which colour? which room?

Red is a rousing, aggressive colour not often used in adults' bedrooms for the simple reason that it is not conducive to restful repose. Yellow is, likewise, not a 'bedroom' colour because it is believed to be over-stimulating, creating turmoil and encouraging intellectual activity – not what bedrooms are designed for. Hotel bedrooms are rarely if ever decorated in yellow, because such rooms apparently prove unpopular with guests compared with, say, predominantly pink rooms. In fact, if you listen to the theorists, there is no brilliant colour that is going to give you a refreshing night's sleep.

The answer to this conundrum is a pragmatic one. If you want to use a bright colour in the bedroom, make sure you surround it with white, pale neutrals or clean pale shades. Limit the bright colour to areas

The red-orange-yellow range of colours is warm yet refreshing (especially when the yellow is included), welcoming and lively. Checks (left) and stripes (on the walls above) provide rhythm and entertain the eye

like wardrobe doors or a section of one wall, and see if you get any sleep. Alternatively, use furnishings and accessories to give the room accents of bright colour – big pillows for reading, for example, or a brilliantly coloured bed cover. Or hang a large bright picture (or a collection of small ones) on one wall.

Red and orange are considered excellent colours for dining rooms and dining areas because, being inherently physical rather than intellectual colours, they encourage the eating and digesting of food (orange is even thought to *make* you hungry). Certainly rich, deep shades of red have been used for centuries in the dining rooms of grand historic houses. In a kitchen, however, red may make things seem too hot for comfort.

Green, being at the centre of the spectrum and also the most common colour in nature, is considered a balancing influence. It is therefore suitable for any room in the house. Blue is likewise a calming colour and immediately provokes images of sky, sea and wide open spaces. The segment of the spectrum containing the cool colours, from blue through green, is popular for kitchens, while yellow, an optimistic and creative colour, is considered a positive influence in a study or home office.

Blue is a popular colour for bathrooms because of its watery associations, and with warm lighting it is not unflattering. However, the most popular colour for bathrooms is white, with its connotations of fresh cleanliness. Accessorising with brightly coloured towels, soaps or pictures can stop a plain white bathroom from seeming clinical.

A white-washed open-air seating area at the home of textile designer Rakesh Thakore in Delhi, India. With built-in benches on three sides, it can be transformed at a whim. At the moment, mattresses and cushions are shades of red, orange and yellow

A good place to start using brilliant colour, if you are at all nervous, is a small room like a lavatory. Bright colour in small spaces bursts upon you joyfully; the rest of this appartment is predominantly white and black

children's rooms

Children's rooms often override these sorts of considerations, being essentially unsophisticated, cheerful spaces designed to be fun and stimulate innocent enthusiasms. Bright red, yellow, orange, purple, blue and green all make appearances in children's rooms, in the form of plastic toys and toy crates, checked or striped curtains and duvet covers, mobiles, painted furniture and garments stacked on shelves or hung in wardrobes.

feng shui

Feng Shui has plenty to say about colour. This is the ancient Chinese science of arranging your home auspiciously to maximise your potential for wealth, health and general happiness. Colour is one of the nine 'cures' that dominate Feng Shui. Every colour has its own distinctive vibrations, which interact with your own vibes to produce an effect on your life.

At the same time, each colour has a theme of its own, many of which are familiar. Thus orange is a sociable colour, suited to someone who likes being in a crowd and pulling together in a team. Yellow has the power of the sun, is stimulating intellectually and represents wisdom and tolerance. In Chinese lore, charms against evil spirits are transcribed onto yellow paper. Green, meanwhile, is linked to the heart and to growth, balance and tranquillity, but too much of it can be a bad thing, reducing you to apathy if it removes all stress. Blue is spiritual, calming and reliable. Purple promotes idealism, imagination and the vision of a higher spiritual level where great deeds may be done, even if this involves sacrifice. Of all

colours in Feng Shui, red is the most auspicious. It symbolises energy, passion, love and joy. It is guileless, direct and emotional. So powerful is it that it should be used carefully to stir up life. There is a danger of over-excitement if you are already a vibrant, emotional person.

When choosing colours for your rooms and spaces, give some thought to your home as a whole. Colour wants to flow around the house, not jolt its way about, unless a sharp shock here and there is purposely designed for effect.

Remember that in a room that does not benefit from direct sunlight, blues and greens will emphasise the chill. Counteract this with warm tones.

This child's room cleverly uses almost every colour of the rainbow whilst retaining a sense of space and serenity. The walls and large blocks of furniture like the sofa are shades of calming blue, the fireplace and other pieces are green, the floor is sandy orange and there are touches of red and yellow, with areas of fresh white. There is no pink and not a frill in sight

which colour? and why?

Getting started with bright colour is like being a child let loose in a sweet shop. There is such a dazzling choice that it is difficult to know where to begin. A world of sensuous pleasure opens out before you, a world that you want to explore and live in for ever.

Unlike a foray to the confectioner's, however, bright colour provides you with a sensation you can live with all day, every day. Once you have allowed yourself the pleasure of learning to look, you will find bright colour almost everywhere. Perhaps I should say 're-learning': think of children's art with its uninhibited use of form and colour. Somewhere on the way to adulthood we become self-conscious and lose the ability to respond to colour in this open, childlike way.

You might think that looking at things is something we all do, at all times except when we have our eyes closed. You would be right, of course, but there are different ways of looking at things. Learning to look, in the way that professional designers and artists do, involves slowing down, concentrating on a subject and analysing it, rather than letting it rush by, giving nothing more than a superficial impression.

The subject might be a single colour in all its nuances, or a composition of colours brought together by accident, a scene in the street or park, or by design, as in a work of art or advertising. In your own home you will find subjects that reward careful looking.

looking at colours

Take a bowl of fruit, for example. Notice how orange the oranges are, how yellow the lemons (much more intense than that wishy-washy yellow so often called 'lemon yellow') and how green or red the apples. Observe how these colours look with each other, how they 'resonate' as they lie together in the bowl. Repeat this experiment with anything in your home that has bright colour, from product packaging to children's toys. Look intensely at these articles, singly and together, and notice not only the qualities of the colours, but also your feelings about them.

Allow yourself to be thrilled
by the yellowness of lemons or
the intensity of the colour of
orange peel, then use that
excitement to decorate your
home. Yellows and oranges are
warm, sunny, juicy

Once you have acquired the knack of looking at colours in this way and take pleasure from their brightness and interaction with other colours, you will notice them everywhere. Suddenly, you will find little scenes that catch your eye and give you pleasure – a white-painted house with bright blue window frames, perhaps, or two children walking together wearing contrasting bright colours. You notice these things and store them up as reference, whereas before you might not have given them a second thought. But don't get too serious – you don't want to lose the thrill of the first impression.

Colour is a vital element of all design, but nowhere more so than in the advertising and product packaging industries, where the impact of bright colour is a serious consideration. Certain colours have well-known effects on the viewer. Yellow, for example, is the most visible of colours and consequently leaps off the shelf at you. Research has shown that it is attractive to people of all ages and both sexes. It has obvious connotations of citrusy freshness and zing, and of accessibility rather than exclusivity, though this changes if you adjust the yellow to gold. The shade of the yellow is important. It must be clean and strong – a greenish yellow is not as appealing to the eye and is definitely not favoured for packaging food because in this context it suggests mould and rot.

The vibrant yellow used in this living kitchen acts as a background, and pulls all the other colours – green, red, blue, even brown – together into a lively and bohemian whole. Even empty, this room echoes with laughter and the enjoyment of good food

Here, yellow becomes sophisticated, throwing into relief the scarlet, black and white of tailored furnishings

flexible yellow

Yellow goes well with many other colours. The combination of colours is an important consideration in the home too, when planning interior decoration. With green, brown and orange it has a country-style look; with black it is sophisticated (but beware the wasp association and keep the black to a minimum); with blue it looks fresh and welcoming. Combining yellow with red and orange creates a hot, fiery look that is reminiscent of high summer, hot countries and sunshine.

All colours are altered in some way by the colours you place alongside them, which is why it is important to plan a whole room together (even if you don't execute the entire scheme immediately). Take bright yellow again, a hugely popular choice in decorating. Yellow with lime green is jazzy and fashionable, but may date sooner than other combinations. Other shades of bright green go well with yellow and can give a spring-like fresh outdoor feeling, but beware of green turning your yellow sour (the yellow needs to be strong and warm to counteract this). With bright red, yellow seems warm and rich, while orange makes it even more brilliant. With purple, yellow's complementary colour, it seems to vibrate and come alive.

getting started

Start your scheme for a room with one colour, then decide whether you want to use it everywhere or sparingly, or somewhere in between – painting just one wall with it, for example. If you don't want it everywhere, you need to decide what your background colour is to be – white, another pale shade or a neutral (see **background and roreground**, pages 100–119).

Use a bright colour on its own, as here (left), where it will go with almost any material, be it shiny metal, mellow wood or a painted finish

Or, as here (right), introduce another colour. Orange and red of similar intensity to the tone used opposite are used to emphasis the strong, flat planes (including the ceiling) of architect John Pardey's home. A lavender blue marks out other architectural areas. The result is powerfully three-dimensional, the colours charming rather than startling

When you have the first colour settled in your mind, decide if it will be the only bright colour, or if you will introduce others. For example, if the main colour for a room is a brilliant sky blue, do you want this on its own, or with another colour – green for a cool effect, perhaps, or pink or red for a more vibrant one? Or do you want other shades of bright blue with it, a slightly darker and a lighter one, for example?

artistic inspiration

One of the most accessible (and enjoyable) sources of inspiration for colour schemes is art. In the years since the Impressionists were inspired by light and colour, encouraged by the scientist Chevreul (see page 35), artists have revelled in bright colour, exploring its possibilities in ever more thrilling ways. There are countless books available showing full-colour reproductions of modern and contemporary artworks, but it is worth taking some trouble to see the original paintings themselves, if the opportunity arises, to appreciate the colours in all their original glory.

There are many artists whose use of colour makes them worth a closer look and you probably have your own favourite. The Post-Impressionists' use of colour continues to thrill, Vincent Van Gogh, Paul Gauguin and Henri Matisse being among the greatest European masters of all ages.

By choosing a scheme of colours from a work of art where the colour relationship has already been established, you are taking a short cut to success. Look at Matisse's paper cut-outs, created late in his life, and see how he uses sharply defined areas of bright colour against white or off-white to superb visual and emotional effect. His blue

White is brilliant too, but it can look blank and empty. A painting that uses a melange of bright colours sings in this all-white interior, giving it meaning and verve

nudes – figures of seated women described in one flat colour only, with no variations – continue to be astonishing in their economy and vibrancy.

Of all the twentieth-century American artists who experimented with colour, including Josef Albers who had taught at the Bauhaus in Germany (see page 29) between 1923 and 1933, the one who produced probably the most sensationally coloured paintings is Mark Rothko. In his huge *Untitled 1952* in the Guggenheim Collection, he places one brilliant yellow against another so that they sing. Painted on a large scale, the colours seem to reach out and embrace you, especially if you stand only a few feet from the surface of the painting. A room in your home offers something like the same scale for using bright colour.

'Op' and 'Pop' artists of the 1960s and since, have used colour in an intentionally sensational way. Bridget Riley excites and confuses the eye with her light-bending optical effects (hence the label, 'Op'), while Roy Lichtenstein depicts cartoon-type scenes on such a large scale that the dots (known as Ben Day dots), which merge on the printed page of a cheaply-printed comic or newspaper, appear individually.

At the end of the twentieth century, artists such as David Hockney and Patrick Heron explored the use of ever more brilliant colour. Looking at their work, a message about colour becomes apparent: it is not only possible to combine bright tones to stunning effect, it can also be easy. Colour is so central to their work that they make its use seems effortless.

going shopping

Besides art galleries and libraries, there are plenty of other accessible sources of inspiration for bright colour combinations. Magazines and catalogues are an obvious choice, as are smart interiors shops and department stores. Interiors shops usually have some areas where sofas, chairs and tables are arranged as they might be in a home. Choose a display of this kind that incorporates an element of bright colour, and take the time to sit down there and relax. Transfer an image of these colours and this style of decorating to your own home.

Crimson and buttercup, with touches of leafy green... the colours in the paintings are repeated in the still life with flowers, fruit and wine on the table

making notes

Look also at details of fabrics, paint and accessories on sale in discerning interiors emporiums. Keep a notebook and write down the details (including the price) of anything that catches your eye – it is very easy to forget exactly where you saw something that you later realise would fit in perfectly with your scheme. Of course, you may not have to look further than your own home for brightly coloured objects to contemplate, in which case try to see these objects anew and decide whether to keep or discard them.

Having a clear-out is an essential part of creating a new style and certainly of changing to bright colour. In order to make space, both physically and in your mind, be brave about parting with clutter that you know deep down is old and tatty. Often, however, all that is needed is a revamp – an old table or lamp can be painted, a chair can have new chushions or covers or simply be concealed with a throw. Some things can find new purpose, as cushions for the garden, for example, or in a different room. If you aren't sure whether you want to part with something, put it in the attic or a cupboard and see if you forget about it. If you do, you may find it is time to give it to someone who actually wants it.

notebooks, swatches and pinboards

Meanwhile, start to collect snippets of bright colours that you like. These could be fabric samples, gift wrapping paper, product packaging, trimmings or paint manufacturers' colour cards. You can organise these by room or by colour, either in a notebook or on large sheets of paper. Pin a sheet up in each of the rooms that you plan to tackle, and staple or stick to it examples of the colours you are considering for that room. This method gives you the opportunity to test how the colours work in the room itself, with a little imagination, and how they will look in different lights. You may like to keep a notebook too, since it allows you to compare colours on the spot when you are in a shop. This is especially useful in the early stages of decorating, before you are ready to promote your ideas to your colour 'pinboard'.

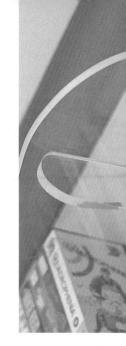

The ultimate fitted kitchen (left). Not a turned oak spindle in sight – almost nothing in sight in fact, since everything is concealed behind sexy green doors and in drawers. The look is futuristic yet organic

Playing the game of colour association can be an entertaining way of researching colours. Think of all the colours you associate with your experiences and life – holidays by the seaside or in exotic locations, your favourite plants and flowers, even colours you dislike because of a link with an unpleasant person or event in your past. Write down your memories and collect examples of the colours connected with them.

Use paint manufacturers' colour cards to make your own colour ring. Display it on white to see the colours cleanly, unaffected by others.

One day you will know you are ready to begin choosing actual paints and fabrics. You will have had enough of research and planning, and will be ready to start transforming a room – or even your entire home – with brilliant colour.

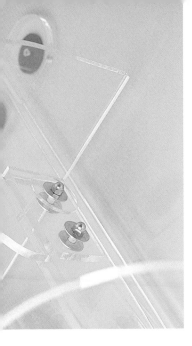

The same kitchen (right) as opposite, showing the meeting of intense bright green with stainless steel. Contemporary decorating revels in the modernity of materials – steel, glass, concrete, wood, and plastics like the shelves above which allow colours to show through

fire and spice

Hot, hot, hot. This palette of reds, pinks and oranges breathes
passion. Glowing with exoticism when seen en masse, these
fruity, summery colours are also cheering when used more
sparingly. They can be grand and historical, dressed up with gilt
and tassels, or contemporary, used to emphasise bold background
planes or to add spice with foreground blocks and splashes

bright accents

Brilliant colour used sparingly draws the eye in an interior that is otherwise white or pale. Flashes of inspired brilliance bring life, an elegant twist or a touch of fun, to rooms which might otherwise seem subdued, sad even. They give focus to quiet, pure interiors. Splashes of vivid red or orange, introduced by flowers or fruit for example, or table linen or trimmings on upholstery, bring warmth to cool spaces

the delft touch

Blue and white is a timeless combination. Fresh and optimistic, it is a classic, reminiscent of Ming ceramics, Delft tiles and schoolgirl gingham, one moment sophisticated, the next simple and unspoilt. Shades of blue recall holidays, the sea, Greek islands and the peeling paint of fishermen's barques. Refreshing, breezy and cool, bright but never gaudy, blue and white will never go out of fashion

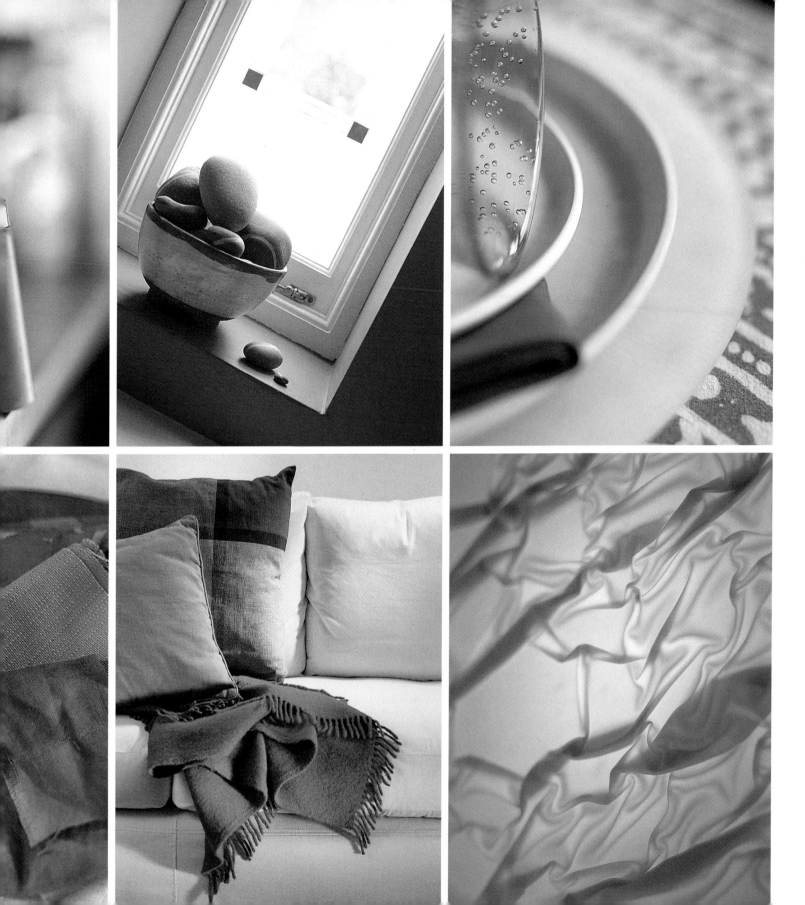

citrus spring

The zing and zap of lemon and lime, tomato and orange, bring sunshine into our homes. Juicy and jaunty, these spring-like colours conjure up dewy mornings, picnics in verdant fields, carefree days when the sap is rising and life feels good. Crisp checks and stripes, cheerful flower prints and fringes – the playful quality of these colours carries through happily to their decorative use in patterns and details

making the most of the shape of your home ❑ large rooms ❑ 'problem'

spaces ❑ painting one wall only ❑ small rooms ❑ 'lowering'

a ceiling ❑ highlighting features ❑ floors

space and colour

dark rooms ❑ cupboards

❑ using colour on a large scale ❑ too much of a

good thing? ❑ linking spaces ❑ defining spaces ❑ coloured glass

(Previous pages) Architect Seth Stein's home in Kensington, London, is a shrine to brilliant colour

(Left) Blue is an obvious and happy choice for decorating a room like this kitchen with enormous windows. Azure links the room with the sky and creates a breezy cerulean atmosphere even when the sun isn't shining

This vibrant green shelving area has a sculptural quality which, added to its dramatic colour, acts as a counterbalance to the length of a galley kitchen

Do you ever have that feeling that you are not making the most of your home? That the rooms look dowdy, their proportions and interesting features not made the most of? Or that something could be done to make the long narrow room seem less like a corridor and the tall, cold room feel warmer? If so, you are not alone. There are few houses and homes without a 'problem' space, one that does not feel right, or that lacks character. Colour, of course, cannot provide solutions to every decorating situation, but it can often help.

large rooms

Take a large, long room, for example. It should be one of the glories of your home, on account of its size, but instead it feels cavernous and unwelcoming. It's great for parties, when it fills up with people and noise, but at other times it seems too big for comfort. Clever use of bright colour will bring the room together and make it feel more welcoming. Start by painting the walls white, or a clean, pale shade, then introduce bright colour on the end wall only – this has the effect of bringing it forwards. Choose a bright blue, green, pink, red or yellow – any brilliant colour that complements the room's contents and furnishings. Hang a few large, bright posters or works of art on the side walls (you can make these yourself in exactly the right colours, see page 134), add a graphic rug on the floor to pull all the elements together and your cavernous space will seem much more inviting.

This technique – painting one wall of a room a brilliant colour – can also be used to frame a particularly interesting view. The ideal colour for this is one that not only complements the decorations and contents of your home, but also ties in or contrasts with the view beyond – whether this be a verdant landscape, a terracotta roofscape or a city scene. Window treatments can create a distraction from a special view, so keep them simple – plain roman or roller blinds, perhaps, or shutters that fold back flat.

small rooms

If you have a room that feels smaller than it really is, colour can help, though you may also need to have

a clear-out to reduce the amount of furniture and possessions you keep there. Paint the whole room white or a pale colour with plenty of white in it, and accentuate the wall through which you enter with a brilliant colour. The result will be a feeling of air and space, but the colour will prevent the room feeling cold or clinical.

'lowering' a ceiling with colour

The traditional way of 'lowering' a ceiling is to paint it a deeper colour than the walls. Beware of using bright colour in this way, however, or you may end up creating the opposite effect by drawing attention to it. Instead, consider painting a generously proportioned band of bright colour around the room at the ideal ceiling height, making sure that it is above the top of any large pictures you wish to hang. This band could be plain, as in the bathroom shown opposite, or could consist of more than one colour – strips of lighter and darker shades of your

The tall walls of this bathroom, right, have been clad with homely tongue and groove boarding – but only up to a sensible height where it is finished with a wooden moulding. Above here, the bricks are bare of plaster and have been painted bright green, which transforms this section of wall into a 'frieze', creating interest where before there was only empty height

A desk formed, left, from two cubby holes in the depth of the fitted cupboards alongside. This extends the space-efficient concept of fitted storage to a working area

chosen red or blue, for example, in order to add interest and movement. You could make a feature of an interesting ceiling, whether sloped or curiously shaped, by using bright colour for emphasis.

Of course, there is no reason why high ceilings should be viewed as a disadvantage (apart from the heating bill, perhaps). On the contrary, they can be magnificent. Paint your walls a bright colour, or colours, right up to the top edge of the walls or the ceiling cornice to emphasise their splendid proportions. Or paint the ceiling a cerulean blue that makes it look like sky on a summer's day. You could even include some birds or butterflies to add a witty note (these could be cut out and stuck on or painted freehand).

highlighting features

Bright colour will help draw attention to any architectural or decorative feature such as a doorway or a window, because it trumpets rather than whispers. If you want to create a focus in a room, consider painting the fireplace or the front wall of the chimney breast a bright colour.

Even better, paint the fireplace one shade – sky blue, for example – and the chimney breast another shade of the same colour. This could be darker or lighter, slightly more green or slightly more purple. This treatment will draw the eye instantly

A steep narrow stairwell (left), potentially gloomy and dull, is painted a glorious blue. Cramped spaces become interesting when painted with vibrant colour

Large blocks of strong colour provided by the sofa and rug (above) prevent this magnificent room from seeming cavernous. The blue fire surround (opposite) illustrates the point about painting a fireplace and the chimney breasts different shades (see text)

to the fireplace the moment you enter the room. If you have the space, group your sofas and chairs around the fireplace (rather than pressing them back against the walls as if in a doctor's waiting room) to create a cosy social space for conversation.

If you are apprehensive about taking what may seem at first to be a drastic step and you are concerned about its success, there are two useful ways of rehearsing the effect. One is to take several photographs of your room, and colour in the appropriate space with felt-tip pens, or overlay a cut-out of brightly coloured paper. The second method is to buy sample pots of the colours you want to try, and paint large sheets of white paper to hang around the room (use the reverse of old rolls of wallpaper or buy inexpensive rolls of children's paper). Unless you intend to use more than one colour on the walls, it is advisable to hang one sheet at a time, or leave plenty of space between different sheets, as your perception of a colour will be affected by other bright colours close by.

transforming floors with colour

Walls and ceilings do not, of course, have a monopoly on colour. Floors, too, can be transformed with brilliant colour. Rug designers already know this, and there are many vibrant contemporary carpets and rugs on the market to brighten up a wooden or other hard floor. Fitted carpet is also available in brilliant colours. There has been an idea prevalent for many decades that bright red or green or blue on the floor will make a room look smaller. On the contrary, it can draw attention to the full size of the room, because the colour leads the eye right to the edge. Fitted carpet in drab or muted shades is safe, but it can drain energy from a room. A bright carpet, on the other hand, can enliven the entire room, giving punch and character.

One thing which cannot be denied about bright colour is

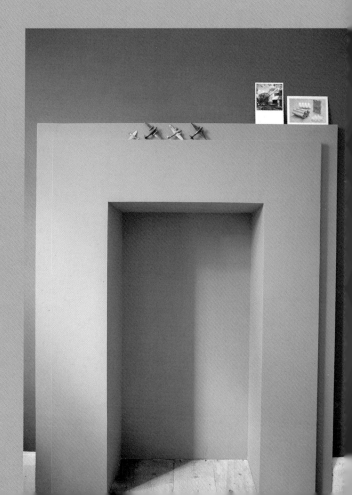

that it has character. Because of this, you can use it to rediscover corners of your home that you had forgotten or discounted. Small spaces such as a hallway or landing, an alcove or the end of a passage, can be transformed from dull emptiness to places with a character of their own. Indeed, if you are at first uncertain about using bright colour, these corners give you an opportunity to experiment on a small scale before planing larger projects.

dark rooms

There is a fear that bright colour will make an already small or dark room feel smaller or darker, and that the solution to lack of space is to paint the walls white or the palest pastel shade. Try this and you will quickly discover that the result is likely to be a chilly space, where you are reluctant to spend any time. Instead, accept that this is a small or dark room, light it well and let planes of juicy colour give it character. Basil Ionides, a fashionable decorator in 1930s London, wrote comfortingly in his book *Colour in Everyday Rooms*: 'Brilliant colour is never gaudy in a dark room'.

cupboards

Ionides had some clever ideas for using bright colour in very small spaces, namely inside cupboards. Paint the inside with crimson or fresh leaf green, or line it with fabric if it is a cabinet for treasures. He suggests the back of bookshelves

The interior of fashion designer Harriet Gubbins' tiny London flat (right) is dazzlingly colourful, and no room more so than the very pink bedroom. Natural light comes only from the skylight over the bed which has built-in storage beneath. Flowers against a fresh garden green (opposite) bring the outdoors in should also be brightly coloured, so that there is a warm glow along the top of the books – warm colours and green are best, he says, rather than cool tones like blue. Practical to the last, he has a word of warning about cupboards with glass doors: 'Remember that a glazed cupboard or shelves need stronger treatment, as the reflections on the glass take off from the colour.'

Large spaces offer opportunities for maximum effect. If bright colour in small spaces glows with the enclosed brilliance of precious stones set in jewellery, on a large scale it has the impact of summer sunshine after a long grey winter. One of the reasons why bright yellow is such a popular decorating colour, especially for kitchens and living rooms, is that it summons up the expansive warmth of sunshine. It makes us feel good, alive. So does burnt orange, which radiates visual heat and reminds us of Mediterranean terracotta.

A large wall, whether in a big room or up a stairwell, gives you a chance to have a bit of fun with colour. You do not

The bright yellow bed (left) is what you notice in this attic bedroom, not the sloping ceiling which is painted white, unifying it with the walls

This sofa is real –
solid, inviting and
very red – a touch-
stone in a dreamy
flat fitted with
translucent walls
and glossy surfaces

Designer-tailor, Ozwald Boateng, commissioned the artist Kevin Allison to decorate his London flat. Red and pink dominate, creating a hot, exotic atmosphere heightened by areas of geometric pattern including this wall of undulating curves reminiscent of dunes and hills (left) and a fireplace of broken chequered shapes (right)

have to use the same colour all over. You could paint three or four wide bands of colour horizontally around the room, or you could grade the colour from, say, blue at one end to mauve at the other, the tone gradually changing along the wall. This latter scheme would take some planning, and probably some mixing of paints, but the effect could be stunning. Such a wall would be a work of art in itself. If, however, you want to hang art on the wall, keep the colour of the wall itself simple so that it does not create a distraction.

using colour on a large scale

This leads to some frequently asked questions in connection with colour on a large scale. Can you have too much of one colour? Can you have too many colours, even if there is plenty of space?

The answer to both of these questions, of course, depends upon your circumstances and definitions.

Yes, you can have too much of one colour, especially if you use it on the walls, floor and all your soft furnishings. The way to use bright colour comfortably in bulk is not to have everything matching, which would be claustrophobic. Instead, either balance the prominent colour with white or a pale colour and introduce small quantities of colours in accessories, or balance it with other colours of similar intensity. The former will create a cooler, more elegant effect, the latter scheme will be exotic and opulent.

If all four walls are brilliant fuchsia pink, for example, have a white ceiling and a neutral or pale floor to define the limits of the pink and refresh it. Your sofa and chairs, if it is a sitting room, could be blue, green,

The brightly coloured stacking chair is one of the decorating icons of the turn of the twenty-first century. The ant and butterfly designs of the 1950s, created by design giant Arne Jacobsen, became fashionable again in the 1990s and inspired similar chairs like these. Stacking chairs save storage space – another contemporary preoccupation

red or white, with further touches of other shades of pink and other colours else-where – in cushions, lamps and pictures. In a dining room, the rich pink will reflect warmth onto a polished table of dark or light wood. Chairs could be wooden too, or a selection of lacquered colours, or covered in plain or patterned contrasting fabric, or they could be painted a colour other than the pink of the walls. White china always looks fine near bright colour, especially on polished wood.

For an opulent effect, use the same pink with red and yellow, and introduce touches of gold with accessories such as gold braid edging on cushions, a gilt chandelier or candlesticks, golden frames around photographs or pictures and brass door knobs. Keep white to a minimum.

too much of a good thing?

Can you have too many colours? Yes, if there is no clear leader and no clear theme. The danger is that too many colours become confused. To prevent this

happening, start with one main colour and add one, two or three subsidiary ones in smaller areas or quantities. Or have two or three well balanced colours and stick to these (refer to the colour wheel on page ooo for more information). If your colour structure is distinctive, small touches of other colour will add interest to the overall appearance of the room, rather than creating muddle. (Think back to Nancy Lancaster's famous yellow drawing room – see page 26.)

linking spaces with colour

Another frequent situation that can create visual confusion or overload is where one room or space leads into or can be seen from another. There are almost certainly such spots in every home and it is worth bearing them in mind when planning

The interior shown on these pages epitomises the best of post minimalist interior design – there's almost nothing in it, but what is there is vibrantly coloured

The cool blue links the dining and sitting spaces, while the deeper blue of the woodwork (in both rooms) is picked up by the cushions on the uncompromisingly red sofa

colour schemes – especially if you want the eye to roam freely from one space into another.

You can use colour connection to link separate spaces, such as a bedroom with an adjoining bathroom. Choose one shade of blue for the bedroom – a dreamy, light shade perhaps, or a green shade approaching turquoise – and another shade of blue for the bathroom, a stronger, seasidy blue that is compatible yet different. Adjoining rooms can be painted in colours that are closely linked – red leading to pink, for example – or that are vibrantly contrasting – red leading to green. Or, link the colour of one room with the accessories of the other. Thus a study leading from a sitting room could be egg-yolk yellow (ideal for intellectual activity) matching the cushions on the sitting room sofa.

defining spaces with colour

Bright colour is ideal for defining separate areas within one space, such as an eating area in a kitchen. Choose either a different colour or a variation of the same colour for the walls of each space and use table linen or china to provide a colour link between the two. Thus a leaf-green kitchen could have a dining area with flame orange walls, with green napkins and green glasses on the table in a similar shade to the kitchen walls so that they provide a visual connection.

utilising coloured glass

Coloured glass is a great asset in contemporary decorating, from glass vessels and objects to tinted glass windows or screens to help manipulate space. Coloured glass has many appealing qualities, in particular its radiance. When light shines through it, it comes alive, casting brilliant colour onto other surfaces. The colour moves and changes as the sun moves through the sky. It makes borrowed light more interesting, and in spatial terms, coloured glass acts as a veil, concealing yet at the same time allowing the eye to travel through it, implying expanses beyond. One part of a room can be concealed – an office with a glass or Perspex screen around it in a corner of the sitting room, for example – without losing the sense of the proportions of the rest of the room.

Replacing the top part of a wall between rooms (at above head height for privacy) with panels of coloured glass will add interest to both rooms. An unappealing view – straight onto a neighbouring brick wall, for example, or across a busy road – can be veiled, and an asset made of the situation. Either hang a glass 'curtain' made from rectangles of coloured glass linked together with metal rings, or strings of large coloured beads, or have shutters made in coloured Perspex. These need not cover the whole length of the window, the bottom half or a central section will do so long as this is enough for privacy or to hide the unattractive view.

The London home of Andrew Jolliffe, advertising copywriter, bursts with colour. A former industrial building, it was first painted white throughout, but this looked chilly and grim, so Andrew painted first one area and then another with brilliant colour. As a result, the place seems filled with life and light. Since this photograph was taken the stair treads have been painted electric blue. The glass vase is contemporary Murano

Blocks of bright colour help to link different areas in the Jolliffes' spacious flat. They considered wooden and galvanised chairs, but opted for these because of their colours which link with other splashes of bright colour elsewhere. Above are the bathroom windows seen opposite

Sheets of toughened coloured glass or Perspex, even sticky-back plastic sheeting, can be used in other places around the house for practicality and effect. An old table could be transformed with a new top, or you can make elegant splashbacks for basins and baths. Spray or paint one side of a clear sheet with waterproof paint in a bright colour (car paint is useful) and, when dry, fix the sheet in place with the painted side against the table top or wall. Perspex can also be obtained with a coloured cut edge.

Panels of plain glass, each covered in a different coloured piece of sticky-back-plastic. Without the colour the owners say these windows looked institutional. Below, zinc sheets are glued to the partition wall. The underside of the bath, floor mosaic tiles and even the soap are all bright red

Coloured glass objects and vessels look spectacular in a modern setting, especially when the sun falls on them or when they are well-lit by artificial light. Display them in a window embrasure, or place them where you can fix a spotlight to shine on them.

Glass panels between rooms can also be decorated. Like panels of one-colour glass, these will add visual interest, veiling what is beyond yet allowing the eye to pass through to the full extent of the space.

the new decorating ❏ modern minimalism ❏ natural colours as partners

❏ colour as highlight ❏ planes of colour as backdrop

background and foreground

light effects ❏ the relationship between

light and brilliant colour ❏ lighting choices ❏ which bulb?

the new decorating

For the best part of a century, the modern architectural aesthetic has favoured white above all other applied colours for interior decoration. In this way of thinking, which dates from the 1930s and is therefore surprisingly old, form and material are everything. Beauty springs from integrity, from the materials' natural colours and textures and from the subtle influences of light, both natural and artificial. Because this modernist idea has been current for so long, it is firmly established in the minds of many professionals, and young architects grow up 'knowing' that it is right. Minimalism goes hand in hand with architectural modernism. It, too, demands purity – it is as much an attitude of mind and a way of living, rejecting all mental and physical clutter, as it is a visual statement. 'Decorating' in this context is almost a dirty word, suggesting surface frippery. A new type of decorating has grown out of the severe aesthetic of minimalism, however, a style that uses form and colour in a way that does not detract from the architecture and materials from which a building is constructed, but that complements and enriches them. You could call this attitude to decorating 'Post Minimalism'.

post minimalism

Instead of the fussy treatments of the 1980s – rag rolling, elaborate floral papers and chintz, swags and tails over windows – which draw attention to themselves, contemporary decorating celebrates the very essence of modern materials. Glass, steel, plywood, concrete, plastics and polymers are all enhanced by 2-D background planes and foreground blocks and details of glowing colour which can be 2-D – pictures or a rug, for example – or 3-D, such as a piece of furniture or an object.

Don't forget that when you paint a wall or object in one flat colour it will not necessarily look the same once the room is lit (see how the shadows alter the tones of sphere and blocks on these pages)

Combining white and natural colours with selective areas of brilliance demonstrates that bright colour need not be overwhelming. On the contrary, it is equally effective (in a different way) when used sparingly, and white is its natural partner. The visual power of a single wall painted verdant green or turquoise can be as great, or possibly greater, than an entire room this colour. The surrounding white concentrates the eye, so that the wall seems to call out: 'Look at me, I'm green!'

Likewise, a white sofa carefully partenered with a collection of small silk or velvet cushions in a single colour, or in red, pink, orange and yellow, or in blues and purples, sings to the eye. You can almost hear the cushions cry: 'Here we are, aren't we beautiful!'. And they are. This is brilliant colour used in the foreground, with restraint, but to impressive effect. A coloured glass vase on the mantle shelf, or tulips in a jug on the table, or a picture which uses brilliant colour can all have this effect in a room that is otherwise white.

In the northern hemisphere an all-white room tends to look grey, especially if it faces north. Even

Plain black and white is handsome and serious but can be severe. Shades of gold in the foreground on bedding, accessories and objects make this bedroom seem accessible rather than intimidating

if it is furnished with neutrals and pastels, these are rarely enough to warm the chill. A few touches of brilliant colour – which could comprise a single section of wall, a large poster, a rug and some cushions – will do the trick, without detracting from the sense of airiness and spaciousness.

background

Background colour can involve literally providing a strong backdrop for a prized object or group of items. Bright colour will bring together a collection of small objects, add interest and throw them into relief if, like white china or carved wooden artefacts, they are not themselves coloured or pale. Painting the insides of cupboards or drawers in which treasures or everyday possessions are kept or displayed makes them more interesting visually and so more appealing to use.

These touches of bright colour, whether part of the room's background decoration or foreground accents, can be used to give vital finishing touches to a room which has subtle decorations. A flame-orange throw over a bed in a room decorated in pale yellow will bring it to life, as will a bright red picture and table napkins in a dining area decorated in pale blue and white, or a section of wall painted purple behind a neutral sofa and chairs.

calming tones

Neutrals – natural flax, calico, pale wood and soft stone – work equally well with bright colours, but with a different result to other colours, including white. Neutrals tone down their brilliance and the bright colours, in turn, give their low-key cousins a subtle lift. Grey, too, works well with brilliant colour, acting as a serene and soothing foil. Some ranges of tone naturally recede (most obviously the subtler blues) and others spring forward (crimson, for example). This is a physiological event rather than simply the workings of the imagination (where blue suggests distant hills and red the apple in your hand), because the eye receives different information from different colours.

The interiors on these two rooms show opposite approaches. On the left, the full extent of the room is emphasised by painting a background section of wall rich red, whilst on the right the large red sofa fills the foreground with its bulky presence. Both rooms have other strong elements – the bulky cupboard on the right, the geometric rug and red cushion on the left

Scarlet and white (following spread): either colour can create a background for the other; in both cases a foreground splash creates contrast and drama

light effects

Colour and light are inextricably linked. In fact, colour is a function of light. There is no perceivable colour in a pitch-dark cave. Only when the lamps are lit do you see the subtle colouring of complex crystalline forms. Every colour has a visual resonance or wavelength, just like radio waves and sunlight. These are part of the same physical pattern. The difference is that the human eye is able to perceive certain wavelengths as colours, though these are limited to a very narrow section of the radiant spectrum.

At one end of this spectrum are radio waves (low energy), then radar, followed by microwaves. Next come infra-red or heat waves, then visible radiant energy (the colour we see) starting with red and ending with violet. After this come ultra-violet waves and x-rays (high energy – they can burn you) at the other end.

The radiant spectrum spans about sixty octaves of energy, of which a quarter are solar energy radiated by the sun 'like a great celestial broadcasting station' (as Maitland Graves said in his 1952 book *Color Fundamentals*). Within these fifteen octaves, only one is visible solar energy, which means that we can only see about one sixtieth of the available radiation in the electromagnetic spectrum.

Strangely, the colour we see on an object is not the colour of the wavelength it absorbs, but colour that the object rejects or reflects when white light falls on it. All the other colours of the spectrum are absorbed into it. A tangerine-coloured bowl is, so to speak, drinking up all the wavelengths of visible solar energy except the tangerine ones. A coloured surface is thus a mirror and

filter, allowing all wavelengths through the filter except the one we see, which is reflected back to us as if the surface were a mirror. When we see pure brilliant white, all the colours of the spectrum are being reflected into our eyes so that we see no colour at all.

how we perceive colour

The human eye is a complex and fascinating organ. Our retinas have many millions of tiny receptors known as rods and cones on account of their shapes. Cones, which are colour sensitive, are concentrated around the optic nerve which leads the information to the brain. Rods have greater light sensitivity than cones but lack ability to detect colour. When you see a colour, the light reflected from it enters the eye through the lens at the front and falls on the retina, where the rods and cones receive the information and transmit it via nerve fibres to the optic nerve. Red is received differently from blue because its wavelengths are shorter, giving it greater visual impact than blue (which really *is* calmer on the eye).

Well-presented coloured glass items are always an eye-catcher in the foreground, especially when lit artificially or placed so that natural light emphasises their glowing colours

Blue and white is a classic combination which is as modern and refreshing as the interior it decorates. Here (left) the bedroom wall is painted a particularly intoxicating shade of intense sky blue which contrasts brilliantly with the dazzling white sheets of the foreground bed and provides a background to Lawrence Llewelyn-Bowen's sensuous painting. A paler shade of blue (opposite) acts as background to objects of a darker blue

A physical reason why bright colours are more exciting than dull ones could be that the 'waves' produced by bright colours are taller or higher. If you visualise the wavelength as a wavy line drawn on paper, its height is the distance between its highest and lowest points – in physics this is called the 'amplitude'. High amplitude colours come from efficient reflectors: dull blue reflects poorly, while bright blue reflects well, with little or no attenuation (reduction in amplitude). If you use a prism to split light into its constituent colours, the colours you see are almost pure, which is to say that you are seeing colours almost without attenuation.

light and bright colour

In physical terms, colour is a function of light. In decorating terms, they are equally inextricably bound, and never more so than when you use brilliant colour. Light and bright colour go together like ripe strawberries and cream. The one has verve, the other shows it up in all its brilliance. Put them together and you have more than the sum of the parts. Indeed, if you use bright colour to decorate your home, you should think of how you are going to light your room at the same time as you plan the colour scheme in order to show it off to its full extent. If you need to employ an electrician to achieve this you naturally want the work done before you apply your white or bright colour to the walls, not afterwards.

Gone are the days of a single pendant bulb hanging gloomily from the ceiling centre. Or rather, they are almost gone – this remnant of primitive twentieth-century domestic illumination still lingers in many

a back bedroom, and elsewhere. It is a reminder of the not-so-distant decades in which electric lighting throughout the house was still considered a modern marvel. Many rooms would have one light only, switched from the door, and the obvious place to put it was dangling in the centre of the room.

lighting choices

Now, of course, lighting has become an industry in itself. The choice of systems, fittings and bulb types can seem thrilling or baffling. The design of lighting has become a vital element in any decorative scheme. The primitive pendant centre bulb is considered ugly and redundant. It should only appear where it has a positive contribution to make, such as in the form of a chandelier or chrome shade over a dining table or a lantern illuminating a stairwell.

First consider how your room is used, since the lighting must be practical. Places where you work, read or eat must have sufficient light to fulfil their functions properly. Then think of the other ways in which you want your lighting to work for you, whether to give general, all-over background illumination or to create atmosphere or provide background radiation by 'washing' or 'grazing'

Yellow in background and foreground. A colour that is at the same time both cerebral and sensual, rich yellow provides a warm, welcoming background in living rooms (far right), and in public spaces like halls and stairwells (above). In bedrooms and bathrooms, by contrast, it is generally confined to foreground details (right)

A collection of aboriginal artworks is enlivened by being presented against this intense yellow, reminiscent of the sunshine in the owner's native Australia. The colour is carried forward onto the sofa upholstery. Woodwork painted purple adds to the richness of the interior

entire walls. You may want it to accent or spotlight specific items or features in the background or foreground, to move (kinetic light), to be a foreground feature in itself (as sculpture) or to be flexible and adjustable, using goose-neck fittings, anglepoises or dimmers.

Lighting can sometimes fulfil more than one function. Working light over a kitchen worksurface, for example, can become background lighting with the aid of a dimmer when you move to the table to eat, still giving you just enough light to enable you to see while serving up the next course, without dazzling the family or your guests. In this situation, the table itself will have its own foreground lighting, perhaps in the form of a dimmable spot supplementing candlelight.

Consider also all the places you can put lights. They could be recessed into the ceiling, hanging from it, concealed by coving or architrave. You can put them on the walls, on tables or set into the floor, or they can be floorstanding, shining up (uplighters) or down. Lighting designers have scented the freedom brought by new technology and have become creative so that you can now buy nets of tiny lights, for example, or floorstanding lamps that are almost sculptures in themselves. New ways of using light are constantly being invented so that artificial light is no longer a utilitarian practicality – it can be fun.

what sort of bulb?

Two other important considerations are the type of bulbs you want to use – which has implications for the colour of the light produced and the amount of energy used – and the type of lamp. Some bulbs are bigger than average (low-energy fluorescents) and some are much smaller (halogen bulbs can be tiny), so take this into consideration when choosing your fittings. Another point which can be significant is heat. Light sources that get hot, including tungsten bulbs, natural sunshine and fire, are called incandescent. Those that are cool, including fluorescent bulbs, are called luminescent.

The conventional, standard light bulb is the tungsten filament bulb. The bulb is hot to touch, its

The same interior as opposite, but this time virulent green walls with yellow woodwork act as a background to ethnic baskets textiles and other art

performance decreases with age and when it blows this is because the filament has worn out or broken. The quality or colour of tungsten light is warm and flattering to human skin tones. Bulbs are cheap to buy, but expensive in the long run because they waste a lot of heat and blow frequently.

Low-energy bulbs are a version of the old fluorescent light that used to be used in long tubes in kitchens but is now generally banished to garages, attics and workshops. These do not have filaments. Instead, the bulb is filled with an argon or krypton gas. The bulb is cool (therefore less energy is wasted as heat) and lasts longer than tungsten bulbs, partly because it does not have a delicate filament. The colour of the light depends on the cocktail in the phosphorescent lining of the bulb – various tones are available – but the ordinary bulb produces whiter light than tungsten. Low-energy bulbs are expensive to buy, but cheaper in the long run because they last about eight times as long as tungsten bulbs.

a popular choice

In 1964 the halogen bulb – or tungsten-halogen, to give it its full name – appeared on the market for the first time . Giving a clean, white light that is also flexible (it can be dimmed, which fluorescent light cannot), halogen lighting is ideal when used with bright colour. The tiny size of the bulbs mean that halogen fitments are often lightweight and discreet. The halogen bulb is the offspring of the conventional tungsten bulb. It, too, has a tungsten filament, but this is suspended in halogen gas. This allows it to burn hotter (and thus brighter, hence the whiteness of the light), and more cleanly so that it retains around ninety-four per cent of its efficiency even towards the end of its life. In turn, this gives it a longer life (two to four times that of a conventional bulb) and means that the filament need only be a fraction of the size of a conventional tungsten bulb (hence their small size). The intense brightness of the light emitted by a halogen bulb can cause problems – dazzle and heat. For this reason, halogen bulbs are often encased in metal diffusers. On the other hand, the intensity of the light they produce can be useful if you want to spotlight individual objects or features. Low-voltage halogen fitments also require transformers (to filter the strength of domestic mains power), but these are now often incorporated into the fitment or are provided as an adjunct to the mains socket and sold with the lamp.

Lighting designers changed gear at the end of the twentieth century – suddenly lighting was sexy and lamps became inventive pieces of techno-sculpture. This one, made from moulded polypropylene, casts interesting light patterns on the wall, formed by its own undulating shape. The colour of the light can also be changed with different 'gels'

There is, of course, another vital form of light in decorating – daylight. Maximise this by replacing curtains with blinds or shutters and use mirrors and gloss paint to reflect and multiply natural light.

the romance of candlelight

Candlelight looks superb near bright colour. It makes brilliantly coloured fabrics glow and adds drama and intimacy to any decorative scheme.

In summary, choose lighting with care, always considering whether you are aiming for background or foreground effects, then enjoy it. Lighting brings colour to life, whether in a whole room or in the corner of the room where you sit to read or stand to prepare food, whether illuminating a single background object or an entire foreground seating or dining area. It can create intimacy or large-scale drama. Above all it should always be safe and practical.

flexibility ❑ types of paint ❑ historic paint ❑ modern hues

❑ different finishes

painted colour

planning ❑ preparation ❑ floors and

other surfaces ❑ revitalising junk ❑ children's rooms

Paint – what wonderful stuff! It is relatively cheap, it's reliable and it's widely available, you can use it on almost any surface and, best of all, it comes in a dazzling array of colours and a variety of finishes. In contemporary decorating, paint is probably the single most useful tool for transformation.

If you want to introduce bright colour into your home, paint is the thing. It can put colour onto your walls and ceilings, woodwork such as window frames and skirting boards, metalwork, floors, furniture and even glassware. You can be daring with paint because if you make a mistake for whatever reason, it is easy and not expensive to correct. Likewise, if you introduce touches of bright colour to your home and decide you want more, which is highly likely, you can add more and more at your own pace. First one wall, then another, then a whole room, and so on.

types of paint

The choice of paints can seem baffling, but basically they fall into two categories: water based and oil based. The trend is increasingly towards water-based paints, which are easier to handle, don't smell so strong, are quick drying and less tiresome to wash out of brushes, rollers and rags because you use cold water rather than white spirit or turpentine. Until quite recently, you had to use oil-based paint on woodwork to obtain a hardwearing, glossy surface. But now, acrylic water-based gloss gives you almost as shiny and durable a finish that will last for many years and possibly as long as oil-based gloss – it hasn't been around for long enough yet to prove itself long-term in the domestic environment.

You also had to use oil-based paints in steamy places such as kitchens and bathrooms, but here too there are now water-based equivalents, specially formulated with chemicals and petrochemical derivatives to make them completely waterproof and washable. Read the label carefully to establish exactly where, how and on what surfaces any given paint can

be used, as well as for other useful information such as coverage, drying time and special cleaning requirements.

The colour in paint is in the form of a pigment, as opposed to dye which is used to colour fabric. As well as pigment, paint contains solvent, binder and usually some additives. The solvent is pure distilled water in water-based paint or a medium such as turpentine in oil-based paint. When the solvent evaporates it leaves behind the other ingredients so the paint becomes hard and dry on the wall. Always buy the best quality paint you can afford, since cheap paint often contains padding or filler. Many paints contain additives, including fungicide to help prevent mildew in kitchens and bathrooms, thickeners to prevent drips in non-drip or ceiling paint, or epoxy resin to improve adhesion in, for example, floor paint.

Binder is possibly the ingredient that most distinguishes historic paints such as distemper from modern paints. In both types, it not only makes the different components of the paint

Go mad with paint. Almost any surface can be painted and offers the opportunity for a bit of colour. The interior on these pages has been transformed gradually – the owners found that once they had a bit of colour, they wanted more, and more! They have used a palette of colours which is lively without being garish

cling together, but also helps the painted coating stick to the wall. In modern paints, the binder is a synthetic polymer medium, usually either vinyl or acrylic, that gives the paint a protective film when it is dry. In historic paints, the binder might be gelatine, gum arabic or, most likely, casein (a milk product derivative), and this is what gives them their characteristic soft, dusty finish. This look is perfect in an old house furnished with antiques, as the colours are appropriately mellow and the surface drinks up light. However, in an interior decorated and furnished in a contemporary style, whatever the age of the building but especially in more modern settings and former industrial locations, modern paints give a finish that is more in keeping

Why confine colour to the interior? The outside of this wooden house is as highly-decorated as the inside, with a similar range of colours so that the spaces are visually linked

with the overall look of the place. They are more reflective and project bright colour much more success-fully. The synthetic plastic-based finish has a flat hardness that is a positive quality in this context.

modern paints

Modern paints come in various degrees of shine – from completely matt, through several degrees of low-gloss with names such as 'silk' and 'satin', to shiny full gloss. Gloss reflects the most light and matt the least. Paints with pearlised and lustrous finishes are increasingly available and popular, as are wallpapers and fabrics with similarly intriguing surfaces. You can also achieve a pearly effect on a wall by painting it with colour then adding a pearlised wash over the top. A specialised product like pearly

The patterns created by the colours on the walls and cupboards of designer-tailor Ozwald Boateng's London flat could almost have come off one of his shirts. His bedroom (opposite) is plain, sumptuous crimson

paint or wash is not cheap, for paint, but the result can be stunning, sophisticated and, to date, relatively exclusive.

making the most of different finishes

Of course, just as you don't have to paint a whole room in one single colour (see page 81), you don't have to use the same finish for every wall – that is, they don't all have to be matt or all silk. If a room is long and narrow, with a window at one end, paint the wall at the dark end with silk or gloss and it will glow with life, especially if it is a brilliant colour. If you have glass-fronted pictures hung on a wall, choose a matt paint for the wall or the effect may be too overwhelmingly reflective.

You can have fun decorating like this, using paints in exactly the same colour but with different finishes. The result will be subtle – some people might not notice it at first – but this method gives you the opportunity to create some dynamic and witty contemporary-looking designs without cluttering the room. You could, for example, paint one wall in wide horizontal or vertical bands or frame a window or other architectural feature using different paint types. You could paint large, graphic motifs like circles of different sizes on a matt wall or ceiling, or you could paint your name or favourite motto in big letters around the top of your bedroom wall.

Glazes are a quick and useful way of achieving a glossy finish on a painted wall. A glaze is like an oil paint without opaque colour, used to enhance the colour behind, rather like lacquer. You can colour clear glaze by adding a spot of artists' oil colour and mixing it well – choose a shade darker than your background colour for added depth and lustre. The best kind of glaze is a slow-drying, oil-based type, which you can make yourself by mixing boiled linseed oil with turpentine or turpentine substitute (the latter with some French chalk or whiting added) in a proportion of three to five. You can buy the ingredients from a specialist decorators' shop or an art materials supplier, who will also probably be able to sell you ready-made glaze.

planning

The choice of available paint colours can seem exhausting, but console yourself with the thought that among them is exactly the colour you want. Decide on a paint range or brand first (which may simply be the one your local DIY store stocks) and stick to it when choosing your colours. The smaller ranges of paint sold by specialist outlets have been developed by a single team or person with the intention offulfilling an overall look, so that any colours you choose should be compatible .

Take your time. Take plenty of colour cards home and cut them up (keeping the relevant reference number or name with each tone) so that you can see each colour on its own, not influenced by the others on the card. If you are still not sure, buy a sample pot and try it out either on the wall itself or on a large sheet of white paper pinned to the wall.

Many DIY superstores and specialist outlets offer a colour matching service. You take in an item in your chosen colour and they put it under a spectrometer which analyses the content of the colour. This mean that you can have almost any colour paint to match things you already have. Buy lots of it (this

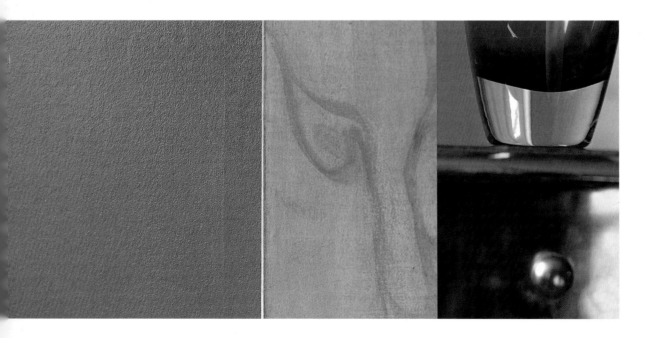

Cooler, deco-inspired colours in the kitchen and living room of Ozwald Boateng's flat. The mural opposite, painted by Kevin Allison, looks like a target. Discs, stripes or shapes of colour can be painted on any wall, either in a contrasting colour or in the same tone but using a different finish of paint – silk on matt, for example

**Silvery metallic paint on a
bathroom wall. Pearlised and
metallic paints and glazes can
be used in any room in the
home, either all over or in one
area only. Here the futuristic
effect is compounded by the
unusual lighting. Is it light, is
it art? Does it matter? Light
meets bright colour in this
Spike Wall Light by Tom Kirk**

goes for any paint) before you start because there is nothing more annoying than having to stop a job
half way through for lack of materials. It is also more expensive to buy paint in small quantities and
sometimes there is a tiny colour discrepancy between different batches.

preparation

The key to good paintwork is always preparation. Whatever the surface, it needs to be clean and sound,
with no dust, grease or loose bits. If you are painting over a shiny surface, like old gloss on woodwork or
metalwork, sand it first to give the new paint something to grip onto and wipe away the sandy bits with a
just-damp cloth or a tack rag before painting.

On walls, use a brush, roller or sponge pad to apply paint in large areas, and a brush for corners
and fiddly bits. If you have a large enough area to justify buying one, a power roller will save time. You
sling the battery-powered pump and paint reservoir (this is heavy when full) over your shoulder and
the paint is forced through a tube to the roller, allowing you to paint acres without interruption. The

disadvantages are that it uses a lot of batteries and it takes time to load with paint and to clean. On the other hand, if you do have a large area to paint it can save you hours. Alternatively, you could buy or hire a paint sprayer.

Before you start painting your walls, it is worth giving them a coat of good-quality acrylic primer. This blocks out any previous colour. This isn't necessary, of course, if the walls are white to start with. It is probable that at least two coats of bright colour will be needed over white, to give good solid coverage. Some special types of paint need one coat only.

Brilliant primaries (above). A blue-painted wall and rich reds on armchair and dress create a renaissance mood. Both bright blue and crimson have regal connotations as well as being seaside colours in a different context. Here they look serious used with velvet, wood and metal

Shades of pink and purple (left and right). Impressive-looking panelling can be constructed from timber or MDF and then painted. Silvery metallic paints and fabrics tone well with blues and purples

painting floors and other surfaces

Concrete and wooden floors can be painted either with ordinary wall paint or with specialist floor paint, which is now available in an increasing number of types and colours. Previously (and this may still be necessary if you cannot find the colour you want) it was necessary to paint floors with several coats of emulsion or eggshell and then several coats of varnish.

If you are stuck with a floor covering that you don't much like or are unable to paint over, you could hide it under a homemade floorcloth. To make a floorcloth, cut a length of canvas or cotton duck to size, allowing extra for hems and shrinkage, and staple or pin to a flat surface. Paint with two coats of acrylic primer, working it well into the fabric, and allow to dry before marking out your design in pencil. Paint your design using emulsion paint, followed by several coats of varnish. The result is a rugged, washable floor covering with a design and colour scheme that tie in with the other decorations in the room. You can draw inspiration for simple, bright designs from late works by Henri Matisse, or from artists of the Bloomsbury Group, such as Vanessa Bell and Duncan Grant. Alternatively, paint simple stripes or quarters in different colours.

Even surfaces like tiles and melamine can now be painted, using specially formulated primer or undercoat that creates a bond for the top coat. Though this is still a fairly expensive exercise (although this depends, of course, on the size of the area to be covered), it is often considerably cheaper than replacing these surfaces completely.

Paints for metal are quite sophisticated in the jobs they can do, killing rust and creating strong, sometimes interesting, finishes. Ever since it was realised that car body spray paints can just as well be used on metal surfaces indoors as on cars themselves, items such as old filing cabinets and the undersides of cast-iron, roll-top baths have been brought to life with brilliant colour.

Plain painted canvases (above) propped up on a shelf introduce blocks of bright colour. They could equally well be hung on the wall

Tables and chairs in a variety of colours, red-orange-yellow (above) and green-blue (opposite). This furniture has had lacquered colour applied by the manufacturers, but you could customise high-street or junk shop finds with a few pots of paint to similar effect

rejuvenating junk

Paint provides probably the easiest method of revitalising wooden and other junk-shop finds, as well as customising items bought in high street and chain stores, whether they be pieces of furniture or objects like trays and boxes. The principles are much the same as for painting walls, in that the surfaces you are going to paint should be completely clean, dry and sound before you start. Use a paint appropriate to the material from which the item is made.

Chairs and small tables are often prime candidates for being painted. These can be brought into any contemporary decorating scheme by being painted white, though dark brown has a vogue with the 'neutrals and naturals' school of decorating. A collection of odd chairs can be unified by painting them the same colour, or cheap high street finds in similar designs can be customised and made to look contemporary by each being painted a different bright colour, or several bright colours between them. The inspiration for this look comes from chairs designed by 1950s gurus like Robin Day, and Arne Jacobsen whose Ant and Butterfly chairs were (and, indeed, still are) manufactured in an exciting choice of brilliant blues, greens, yellow, red, oranges and other colours.

creating your own art

Don't forget the existence of dead flat oil paint when choosing a finish for furniture. This is essentially an old-fashioned paint that looks great in the modern context. It is completely matt (hence 'dead flat'), with a soft, milky finish that wears beautifully. Because it is not gloss, it does not have the same protection against greasy fingers and other agents of distress, but this can be one of its charms if you like the weathered look. You could always use gloss on the table top for durability, with everything below painted in dead flat oil.

If you are artistically minded, or simply on a severe budget, and are short of original art to hang on your walls, you can always make your own brightly coloured paintings. Buy canvases that are already stretched and primed from an art materials supplier, or simply paint directly onto a white wall using emulsion. Paint three bright flat colours onto three separate canvases, two of them half the size of the other, and hang them either as a single unit, in a square or rectangle, or in a row. Alternatively, you could paint the same colours directly onto the wall, having first measured and lightly drawn the outlines. If you feel really ambitious, you could paint a whole wall in this way, effectively creating a mural. Paint it on sections of board or large canvasses and you can easily take it with you when you move, or remove it or paint over it when you feel like a change.

You can have fun creating art on canvas. Look at paintings by Josef Albers, Jackson Pollock, Craigie Aitchison, Bridget Riley or any other artists that catch your eye as you wander around your local galleries or browse through books in the modern art section of your library. Use colours in your canvases that appear elsewhere in the room, or different, compatible colours if you want to create a frisson.

children's rooms

Children's rooms cry out for bright colour, which is easily and cheaply provided with paint. Children have surprisingly definite ideas about colour from a young age – those that they like and those that they don't – though, like adults, they can be pleasantly surprised when actually faced with a colour on the 'not' list. Ask a child what she or he wants and try to provide it – either all over or on one wall only – to mutual delight. If two or more children are sharing a room and want differ-ent colours, one solution is to paint the room

white and accent sections of the wall with colour – blocks of colour behind a bookcase, behind the bunk beds, around the fireplace or on the toy cupboard. So long as there are large areas of white (the ceiling for a start) the effect should not be overwhelming. On the contrary, it will be fresh and vibrant.

Utilitarian children's furniture like beds and cupboards made in softwood can be customised with paint (if the furniture was flat-packed, make sure all the screws are thoroughly tightened before you paint over them). Melamine and veneered furniture can be painted too, using the correct primer. If the furniture was brown, paint it all white first for maximum brightness in the colour you are going to paint over it. Leave narrow strips of white between the bright colours to maximise their brilliance.

The colours of this child's room are taken from the illustrations of the classic Barbar the Elephant books (left). A soothing green acts as a backdrop to splashes of other colour. The buttons of the upholstered red chair (above) pick up all the other colours in the room (see page 39 for a close-up)

finishing touches ❑ changing your rooms by season ❑ floors

patterned colour

tiles ❑ fabrics ❑ presonalising textiles

finishing touches

Your decorating scheme is now complete – or almost. You have brilliant colour on your walls, or they are white or a pale colour that complements the bright furniture, furnishings and artworks. Your flooring is chosen, be it brilliantly coloured carpet, linoleum or a painted finish, or natural wood or matting as a background for bright rugs. What else is there to add?

This is the moment to think about pattern. When the basics are laid down – the solid planes and blocks of colour on the walls and floor and the important furniture – this is the time to sit back and let your imagination run riot. Patterned colour can bring added energy, a bit of zip and zap, to your decorating scheme. This is an opportunity to have some fun.

Like every element in your scheme, pattern in the form of fabrics, china, rugs and throws can be expensive, but it doesn't have to be. There are ways of introducing pattern cheaply, and because it is added after the basics, there is no need to hurry. You can add pattern when you see something that appeals, you can acquire something you have saved up for, or if you are on a severe budget you can make or decorate something yourself.

Once you have established the basic structure and colour for your room, have some fun adding pattern. This teapot was given to fashion designer Harriet Gubbins by a friend who guessed she would love its crazy surface sparkle, its brightness and gaiety. It isn't just for show – it brews a heady cuppa

One of the advantages of patterned items such as cushions, curtains and loose covers is that you can change them to suit the current fashion, season or simply your mood. Curtains that are suitable in summer – unlined floaty sheers, for example – can be replaced in winter with something more substantial. You can even vary the colour scheme at the same time – choosing warm, pimento shades in winter and cool seaside blues and violets in summer.

changing rooms

Cushions and throws offer endless opportunity for pattern and change. You can make cushion covers yourself at little cost, especially if you use an inexpensive fabric on the reverse. On the patterned side, you can introduce different textures by weaving ribbons, knitting stripes, creating appliqué or patchwork or sewing on coloured buttons. If you have a particular theme in your room, consider using samples or reproductions of vintage cloth from the 1950s, 60s or 70s or antique linen. For an opulent effect, cover cushions with luxurious velvet or glossy silk. Throws can be sewn, knitted or crocheted (ask your Granny to make one for you), or you can dye a dustsheet or simply use a colourful tablecloth or vibrant woven blanket.

Decorate the established elements of your home like walls and ceilings with a changing picture show. A projector will display blocks of colour or images which you can change at will

You can also add pattern to elements of the room that are already established, using a projector or light box. A projector will give you regularly changing images of any subject of your choice, as will wall-mounted light boxes, though these images remain the same until you replace the transparency.

If you want a more permanent effect, create a frieze around the top of the walls you have already painted and finished. Gone are the days when you might have been tempted by a frieze consisting of a flowered print on a narrow strip of paper. Today, you want something simpler, more sophisticated and more generous in proportions. Start by painting a band of colour around the top of the walls – 10 inches (25cm) wide or more. Then design a bold repeat pattern to fill the space, perhaps using stick-on elements at intervals to punctuate the pattern. These could be 3-inch (7.5-cm) squares of mirrored glass, nuggets of coloured glass or pretty pebbles you have collected on the beach.

For a more continuous effect, create a linking design of zigzags or interlocking curved lines, using metallic paints or silver leaf. Draw the design lightly in pencil first, if this will increase your confidence, and then paint over the pencil marks. If you are working with silver leaf, first paint the pattern with size

Even the coolest all-white or neutral interior benefits from an injection of colour. In a London home this is provided by patterned, beaded North African neckpieces (left) alongside furniture and objects by the latest western and eastern artists and designers

Architect Dale Jones-Evans has chosen a predominantly white scheme for his home in Sydney, Australia (right), with strong blocks of geometric pattern on sofa and opposite wall

and then rub on the sheets of metal while the size is still tacky. Materials such as these can be bought from an art materials supplier.

If you are nervous about applying pattern freehand to a large area such as this, you may prefer to stamp a repeat pattern onto your coloured border. You can buy rubber stamps in a variety of patterns and sizes from DIY stores, or you could design and cut your own from lino. Graphic motifs like stars and moons, leaves, spirals or, for a bathroom or child's bedroom, boats or shells, work well. Keep the design simple, graphic and stylised. Too much detail will look fussy and won't be appreciated from eye-level.

Stencils and sponges are still around and can be useful tools. The designs of ready-cut ones tend not to be in keeping with contemporary decoration – bunches of flowers, ribbon bows and so on, so be careful which you choose, or make your own.

Wallpaper is the traditional way of adding all-over pattern to your walls. In general, patterned wallpaper tends to be retrospective or fussy. Most wallpaper is not in keeping with the modern look, which is clean, sharp, smooth and definitely unfussy. Paint gives a better fresh, flat look and it is cheaper. However, there is a small selection of wallpapers which is forward-looking, some with metallic and pearlised finishes in parts of the design, and the patterns themselves are geometric or highly stylised.

floors

Floors provide an often-overlooked opportunity for pattern with a contemporary edge. Hard floors like concrete and wood can be painted in any pattern you like. All-over colour and pattern painted freehand are quicker and more fun, and nobody can say that you've gone wrong if a circle isn't perfect. Consider where the furniture is to go and design your floor pattern accordingly.

Rugs are an asset in contemporary decorating, introducing splashes of bright colour in a way that can have the miraculous effect of pulling together a room that previously felt unfinished or unsatisfactory. Group your sofa and chairs around a luxurious pile rug or an exotic kilim (the latter can also be used as a door covering, curtain, throw or be draped over a table) and the room will have a focus.

Tableware and china can add pattern to an interior. A hand printed indigo table cloth (right) is here teamed with glass and china in other shades of blue

The yellow and green of table mats woven in a chequered pattern (left) are picked up by china and table linen. Each place around the table could have a different colour theme

Natural floorings such as coir and seagrass provide an attractive background to rugs, especially the smoother types which are kinder to rugs over time. If your floor is covered with one of the rougher, hairier types of natural flooring, make sure you use a suitable underlay for your rug and avoid laying one that is delicate or especially valuable.

Persian and other oriental rugs and kilims can also be found in bright colours, though they are most famous for their traditional rich, mellow tones. Turkish and Caucasian rugs, and some Persians, often have areas of brilliant red. There is a relatively new type of Persian rug (countries other than Iran make them but they are generally poor, and often drab, imitations) called the 'gabbeh'. Gabbehs allow the craftspeople who weave them to express themselves free-form, without the constraints of age-old designs, in colours that are often bright and exciting.

Pile rugs and kilims are made today in stunning bright colours and these can be seen in the bazaars and nomads' tents of Iran, but such rugs rarely reach the western market because they are not perceived to be what the western customer wants. Of all the Persian rug types, the gabbeh is the obvious choice for bright colour on your floor, especially with contemporary furniture and furnishings. If you are good with your hands, you can of course create your own tufted or rag rug, basing your design on an abstract work of art in bright colours that appeal to you.

A chair by Heinz and Bodo Rasch (left) stands on a 1960s rug in the home of Jane Collins, whose shop Sixty 6 in London is renowned for its stock of original 1950s and 1960s pieces. The home of artist Kate Blee (right), uses a 'Circle' rug by Christopher Farr, to introduce colour and pattern into an otherwise monochromatic interior

Floor tiles introduce hardwearing areas of bright colour and pattern. These could be linoleum, which has shaken off its dusty image and is now available in some glowing colours. Or the tiles could be ceramic, or painted or stained plywood or cork, protected with layers of yacht varnish. Paint or stain your tiles in different colours *before* laying them, to make the job easier.

tiles

Tiles have traditionally been used in wet places like bathrooms and to provide splashbacks for basins and sinks around the house, to prevent walls getting wet. Rectangular tiles, arranged either flat or up-ended, look contemporary. You could use tiles of one colour only, creating a block. If the tiles have been glazed by hand there will be sufficient variation across their surfaces for the block of colour not to seem monotonous. Or you could use a high proportion of plain white, with three or more other bright colours within a local tonal range – blues and purples, for example, or reds and oranges with some rich yellow – scattered through them. Tile mosaic, too, can introduce cheerful bright colour.

fabric

Textiles and fabrics not only bring colour and pattern to an interior, but also a fluidity which can be effective. Above all, they can bring texture, which is such an important element of 'post-minimalist' decorating. Sometimes the pattern is in the texture, as in herringbone and other decorative weaves, cable knit cashmere or wool, or printed velvet.

There are many patterened fabrics of classic design that are brightly coloured and can make a contribution to the contemporary interior, such as Provençal prints with their searing reds, greens, blues and, above all, their typical brilliant egg-yolk yellow.

Tile art. These little pieces of fired ceramic are among the most ancient devices for decorating buildings, and still among the most practical. Damp rooms like kitchens and bathrooms (left, above and opposite) cry out for tiles, where they can introduce some colour and pattern

Textiles add pattern and texture in the form of curtains, covers, throws, cushions and other soft accessories. A buttercup yellow blanket (left) is finished with lavender blue yarn; a glossy brocade (right) adds sophistication

Other classic patterned fabrics can sometimes be bright and colourful, such as tartans and plaids. Some of the traditional Scottish tartans, including the Buchanan with its bands of yellow, scarlet and green and Cameron of Lochiel with navy and green stripes crossing a red ground, are fine examples of this and have inspired fabric designers to create new designs using simple, perpendicular lines of colour overlapping and repeated at intervals. Many of these are woven in wool, as are real tartans, but some are woven in or printed onto other fibres, most effectively crisp cotton.

International trade brings us many wonderful things, not least a wide variety of vibrant ethnic fabrics from around the world – many with wonderful printed or woven patterns. The borders of silk saris are often gloriously exotic, using gold, silver and other coloured threads. Among the most astonishing ethnic patterned fabric is ikat, the name referring to a complex dyeing technique used primarily in areas such as Central America, the Far East and Indonesia (from where it came to Europe via the Dutch settlers).

In the ikat technique, the yarn is dyed in a complex pattern before being woven into cloth. This method involves tying the bundles of yarn tightly, before dropping them into the dye, so that they resist the dye in places. This process can be repeated several times, each time the yarn being tied in a different place and a stronger dye being used. Only when the multicoloured yarns are woven is the great skill in the tying revealed, because as the weaving progresses a pattern emerges on the cloth – a pattern which was calculated before the tying of the bundles began. On the cloth, the design is clear but its edges are characteristically blurred.

Fabric like this is produced by hand with labour intensive techniques. At the other end of the scale are the machine-produced creations of the western world and developed countries. Here, the most interesting innovation is in the use of pearlised and iridescent patterns. Due to the complex production processes, many of these fabrics are fairly expensive.

the personal touch

Of course, you don't have to buy mass-produced patterned fabrics. You can personalise plain fabric, either coloured or pale, by drawing or painting your own brightly coloured pattern onto it using fabric pens or paints or by appliqué – sewing on a design of other pieces of fabric. Use motifs that occur elsewhere in the room or that refer to you or the setting of your home, like boats or sea creatures if you live within sight of the sea. Motifs can be drawn from any other pattern in the room – patterns on glass or china, on a cushion or woven into a rug. Alternatively, you could use a personal symbol, such as your initial or something that indicates it – a bee if your name begins with the letter 'B', for example. Practice your

design first on paper. You can also create relief designs by painting bleach onto plain coloured fabric. This usually works best on natural fibres, and you should always experiment first on a spare piece of fabric to test the success of the method before starting.

Yet another way of creating unique brilliantly coloured fabric is, of course, to dye your own. One method of making completely original curtains is to use cold water dyes in two colours that go well with your decorative scheme. Take a length of sheer or translucent fabric like muslin or lightweight calico (make sure you wash it first to remove surface dressings) and dip one end only into a bucket or basin of the dye. Hold it straight and steady so that the dye can creep evenly up the fabric and remove it when the dye has covered your chosen area. When the first area is dry, do the same with the other end, either leaving a pale, undyed band in between, or immersing the fabric so that the two colours just meet in the middle. You can repeat the process on smaller pieces of fabric for cushion covers or table napkins.

Dyes and brightly coloured fabrics are so easy to obtain today that we often take them for granted. But it was barely a 150 years ago that the breakthrough into modern dyes was made by an Englishman, William Henry Perkin. Even then the aniline dye he discovered proved to be fugitive and unsatisfactory.

As well as colour and pattern, textiles accessories can lend a note of glamour to an interior. The delicate pearly edging on a sunny yellow sari (left) is subtle and seductive; luxurious weaves on ethnic fabric and rugs (right)

Dyeing is thought to have originated in India and the Far East thousands of years ago, the dyestuffs being derived from anything found in the natural world that could do the job, such as leaves, berries and insects. One of the properties of a dye is, by definition, that it should be soluble – and this is before you face the problem of getting it to bond with the fabric, for which an agent or mordant may be required. Solubility distinguishes dye from pigment, which is a colouring material made up of tiny solid particles that lie across the surface of the item they are colouring, rather than binding with it to become one.

Domestic clothes-washing machines make so much possible, including hot-water dyeing at home. Cold water dyes have become sophisticated, as have brightly coloured pens for drawing patterns onto fabric, so that dyeing, including tie-dyeing is now something we can all have fun doing at home – whether it is customising ready-made items or creating new ones entirely our own. If your pastel loose covers get marked by children and dogs, simply dye them fuschia or saffron, cerulean or cyan blue – the names alone transport you to another world, of exotica, of excitement, of brilliant colour.

Jan Milne, whose textile prints are shown on the cushions in these pictures, is one of many contemporary designers who extol the joys of brilliant colour through their work. Like Verner Panton, the venerated Danish twentieth century designer of furniture and furnishings, they know that colours 'can generate an echo in the soul and influence the entire body'

index

acknowledgements

Making this book has been a fantastic experience, due not only to the thrill that comes from working with bright colour, but also to the enthusiasm and efficiency of Kate Oldfield and the team at Kyle Cathie, Paul Welti the book's designer and Ray Main the photographer and his assistant Owen, all of whom I thank heartily. My thanks also to Mandy Aspinall, Lucy and Zac Barratt, Ozwald Boateng, Felicity Bryan and her team including Michèle Topham, Jane Collins, stylist Karina Garrick, Felicity Green, Heather & David Hilliard, Jo from Purves &

Purves, Andrew & Miranda Jolliffe, Richard Lacy from Falkner Ceramics, Jan Milne, William Selka, Stuart from GTC and all the people whose houses we photographed.

Elizabeth Hilliard

All photography by Ray Main of Mainstream, except for the following: Stephen Brayne p 150; Richard Bryant/Arcaid pp 29, 63, 78-9; David Churchill/Arcaid pp 100-1; Georgie Cole/Arcaid p 145; Richard Waite/Arcaid p 148; Andreas von

Einsiedel/National Trust pp 24 & 25; Tim Street-Porter/ Elizabeth Whiting Associates (EWA) pp 6-7 & 120-1; Rodney Hyett/EWA pp 12, 15 & 16 (x2); Di Lewis/EWA p 12 (x2); David Markson/EWA p 12; Andreas Von-Einsiedel/EWA p 14

The publishers have endeavoured to get permission to reproduce all the photographs in this publication. If we have unwittingly overlooked any, we sincerely apologise and will be pleased to rectify the situation in all forthcoming editions.

contacts and addresses

Kevin Allison [Artisan.K.]
(see pages 90, 91 & 126-129)
31 All Saints Road
London W11 1HE
+44 (0) 171 243 4149 (tel/fax)

Babylon Designs
Unit 7
New Inn Street
London Ec2A 3PV
+44 (0)171 729 3321

David Mellor
4 Sloane Square
London SW1
+44 (0) 171 730 4259

Falkner Ceramics (see page 150, right)
Contemporary ceramics for gardens and interiors. Commissions welcomed.
1 Brierley Road
Balham
London SW12 9LY
+44 (0) 181 772 0070

Farrow & Ball (see pages 48 & 51)
London showroom address:
249 Fulham Road
London SW3 6HY
for enquiries call +44 (0) 1202 876 141
for USA enquiries,
call Christopher Norman Inc.
+1 212 647 0303

General Trading Company
144 Sloane Street
Sloane Square
London SW1X 9BL
+44 (0) 171 730411
other branches
Bath +44 (0) 1225 461 507
Cirencester +44 (0) 1285 652 314

Habitat UK
Press Office
The Heals Building
196 Tottenham Court Road
London W1P 9LD
+44 (0) 845 601 0740

Kappa Lambda Rugs (see page 98)
Unit 8
Regis Road
London NW5 EW
+44 (0) 171 485 8822

Jan Milne [textile designer]
(see pages 156 & 157)
Unit 19 Govan Workspace
Six Harmony Row
Govan
Glasgow G51 3BA
Scotland
+44 (0) 141 445 5554 (tel/fax)

Purves and Purves
80, 81 & 83 Tottenham Court Road
London W1P 8HD
+44 (0) 171 580 8223